A HISTORY OF BURLEY TOBACCO

IN EAST TENNESSEE & WESTERN NORTH CAROLINA

BILLY YEARGIN *with Christopher Bickers*

THE History PRESS

Published by The History Press
Charleston, SC 29403
www.historypress.net

Front cover, top: Burley fields during harvest, near Vilas, North Carolina. *Photo by Joe McNeil.*
Bottom: A burley-growing couple in Greene County, Tennessee. *Photo by Bob Hurley.*

Back cover, top: A contemporary barn near Lafayette, Tennessee. *Photo by Chris Bickers. Bottom*: A
traditional barn near Weaverville, North Carolina. *Photo by Chris Bickers.*

First published 2015

Manufactured in the United States

ISBN 978.1.62619.960.6

Library of Congress Control Number: 2015931114

Notice: The information in this book is true and complete to the best of our knowledge. It is
offered without guarantee on the part of the authors or The History Press. The authors and
The History Press disclaim all liability in connection with the use of this book.

CONTENTS

PREFACE

When Clisbe Austin and Silas Bernard, two farmers from the Greeneville, Tennessee area, brought the first burley tobacco seed to Greene County in 1887 and convinced other local farmers to plant it, they probably had no idea that they had launched a commodity that would form the backbone of the agricultural economy in the region for over one hundred years.

Now, though burley tobacco seems to have passed its peak, it still is an important part of the lives of hill country farmers. In this book, we have tried to document this dramatic story through historical investigation but more particularly through the words of veteran burley growers who place the dry historical facts into a human perspective. We have also included a section on growers' efforts to ensure a stable market for their product, a section on the effects of deregulation of burley marketing and a history of the university research station in Greeneville. In addition, we have included a bonus section on the history of the auction market as a means of selling all types of tobacco.

We hope you enjoy it. We have received a great deal of assistance from a number of sources, most especially from the Burley Stabilization Corporation and its chief executive officer, Daniel Green, and president, George Marks. Green's predecessor, the late Charles Finch, helped considerably in the development of the project and is remembered gratefully. We also thank the staff of the University of Tennessee Research & Education Center at Greeneville for all the assistance it has provided.

Let's include two sad notes: One of our featured farmers—Johnny Shipley of Greene County, Tennessee—passed away before this book made it to the printer. Additionally, one of our contributors, Bob Hurley, also of Greene County, died unexpectedly before he was able to write the piece he planned to do for us. But he contributed several fine photographs. We were very happy to meet both in connection with this book, and both will be missed.

1

THE BIRTH OF BURLEY IN THE HILL COUNTRY

It is not the only type of tobacco ever grown in the foothills of the Appalachians and the headwaters of the Tennessee River. It wasn't even the first. But when burley—or white burley, as it was called back then—made its appearance in the 1880s, it quickly displayed characteristics that made it a near-perfect cash crop for farmers in the mountains, ridges and valleys of east Tennessee, southwest Virginia and western North Carolina.

And that wasn't its geographic limitation. Indeed, the history of tobacco in these states is one of burley slowly migrating from the hills to the central basin of Tennessee, where it has taken its rightful place in that area's agriculture.

But let's go back to the beginning. A cash crop was mightily needed in the late nineteenth and early twentieth centuries in the hill country. Except for the occasional dairy farm, there was hardly any agricultural enterprise that could generate cash for off-farm purchases in this area, characterized as it was by small farms, small fields and, in many cases, steep slopes.

But other types of tobacco just didn't fill the need. Dark tobacco was grown extensively in the early years. And for fifteen or twenty years near the end of the nineteenth century, hill country farmers tried hard to make flue-cured tobacco work in this environment. They weren't able to, but as the twentieth century got started, more and more of them enjoyed success with burley.

Two boys and a goat enjoy a break from tobacco in Greene County, Tennessee, in the early 1970s. *Photo by Bob Hurley.*

Robert Shipley of Watauga County, North Carolina, a farmer who was born in 1912 and remembers that era better than almost anybody, describes the economic situation at the time.

"Before burley arrived, most of our people were employed in what we would call subsistence farming," he said in interviews in 2011 and 2013. "They were self-sufficient in food and produced pretty much what they ate. They killed hogs for their meat supply and would sometimes kill cattle for beef. Everybody had a garden, and it was standard practice to preserve and can produce. Sometimes you didn't have to do even that. You could keep potatoes and cabbage for a long period of time just by burying them. So our folks didn't go hungry: they just weren't used to having a lot of money."

That changed after farmers learned about the potential of burley. It soon proved to be the only realistic choice as a cash crop, says Shipley. "We didn't have any other dependable cash crop in this area. That was the big reason that burley spread in the mountains."

But adoption wasn't immediate, Shipley remembers. It didn't really get going until a federal program was developed to stabilize production and marketing: "It led to an increase in price, so that farmers who grew it had some money left over after paying their expenses of growing tobacco. It was a good change, definitely. From that time, tobacco paid taxes and supported the schools and churches of this land."

For all practical purposes, the new white burley didn't appear in the Tennessee-Carolina-Virginia hill country until 1887, when two farmers, Clisbe Austin and Silas Bernard, procured some of the new seed and brought it to the Greeneville area. They convinced many of the local

A burley-growing couple shows pride in a good crop in Greene County, Tennessee, in the early 1970s. *Photo by Bob Hurley.*

farmers to plant burley rather than attempting to compete in growing flue-cured tobacco with growers in North Carolina and other states to the east. But flue-cured was in much greater demand than burley, and up until 1916, burley plantings were largely limited to Greene and Washington Counties. After that, when demand for burley was spurred by the popularity of the Camel brand cigarette, its growth spread throughout most of the state.

It eventually reached the dark tobacco–producing areas of middle Tennessee. George Marks of Clarksville, Tennessee, remembers, "This area traditionally produced dark tobacco, but we didn't start producing burley until after World War II. Burley came here at a good time. So many farmers were looking for an alternative to dark tobacco, and a lot took up burley then. If you wanted to make [up] for the loss of dark demand or to expand, it was the only way."

"It became a stable factor in the economy all across the state," said the late Johnny Shipley of Chuckey, Tennessee, in an interview before his passing. "Without burley, it would have been hard to keep the farm in the family," he said. "It was the only big cash crop we had. It was your Christmas money, it was your back to school money, it was your shoe and clothing money."

Bill Harmon of Sugar Grove, North Carolina, says, "It was the one crop you could just about be certain you would get rewarded on. In 1973, I made enough off an acre of tobacco to buy a tractor in one year. How much was that? I gave $3,600 for the tractor. I may have had a little left. Tobacco was mighty good to us."

In the deregulated economy of the twenty-first century, some younger growers are less optimistic than their fathers might have been. "I don't know how confident I feel about the future of tobacco in this area because of the labor issue and because costs are so high and input costs absolutely are not decreasing," says David Miller of Abingdon, Virginia.

Kenneth Reynolds, also of Abingdon, puts it all in perspective: "Forty or fifty years ago, everybody made money growing tobacco; it was just a matter of how much you got paid. Today, it is a matter of survival of the fittest.

When the federal government ended the supply control program for tobacco in 2004, there was considerable concern that burley might disappear from the hill country altogether, and maybe from the rest of Tennessee as well. What a catastrophe that would have been—like Mississippi without cotton or Iowa without corn. But that hasn't been the case. Some farmers have gotten out of the crop, a few have gotten in and many have gotten bigger. There has definitely been a change in location. Greene County, for many years, was the leading burley producer in these three states, but now

Macon County near Nashville is by far the leader. But that just shows that these states still have plenty of resources when it comes to growing this type of tobacco. It seems safe to say that as long as the world wants high-quality tobacco, burley will be grown in Tennessee, North Carolina and Virginia.

Where Tobacco Culture Was Born

It should be noted that burley in Tennessee descends by a direct line from the tobacco that was developed by Jamestown colonist John Rolfe, and many of the practices that Tennessee's early tobacco growers used were perfected in the fields of central Virginia in the seventeenth and eighteenth centuries.

As described by Lee Pelham Cotton, park ranger at the Colonial (Virginia) National Historical Park in Williamsburg, the Jamestown colonists soon learned to grow seedlings in beds covered with pine boughs. They would be set in the field in knee-high hills spaced every three or four feet using a hoe. "This task was considered the most arduous one in the tobacco cultivation

A costumed reenactor at the Jamestown (Virginia) Settlement Park demonstrates how America's first tobacco farmers planted their tobacco in "hills" created with a hilling hoe. *Photo by Chris Bickers.*

Of all the pests in the tobacco of Jamestown, the most feared was the hornworm. These two reenactors show how the colonists would scout for it. *Photo by Chris Bickers.*

Ensuring that the water requirements of young tobacco plants were met would have been a top priority for the Jamestown colonists. *Photo by Chris Bickers.*

process," Cotton says. "An experienced adult could prepare no more than five hundred hills a day."

Until the plant reached knee height, weekly cultivation was necessary to deter both weeds and cutworms. "The work was done both with a hoe and by hand, the hills around the tobacco being reformed at the same time," says Cotton. When the leaves were ripe, the plants were cut with a sharp knife between the bottom leaves and the ground.

In the first few years of tobacco cultivation, the plants were simply covered with hay and left in the field to cure or "sweat." This method was abandoned after 1618, and growers chose instead to hang the leaves on lines or sticks, at first outside on fence rails and later in barns.

BURLEY IN THE HILLS

Throughout its history and growth, tobacco has played an important part in the development of Tennessee, southwestern Virginia and western North Carolina. Its seeds arrived with the first settlers. Its cultivation spread rapidly throughout the area. It became the livelihood for thousands of farm families in the three states. Tobacco culture has created jobs in manufacturing, processing and numerous other industries related to the tobacco industry. Tobacco sales over retail counters have added millions of dollars in excise taxes to both state and federal treasuries. The development of tobacco in Tennessee and its eastern neighbor states closely parallels that of Kentucky. Both states shared the growth of the three main types of tobacco cultivated in that part of the country—dark air cured, dark fire cured and the light air cured–type burley. But of these types, burley—which we probably ought to call "white" burley—became and continues to be the most widely cultivated type in Tennessee, western Virginia and North Carolina.

The dominant type of burley before the American Civil War was a dark air cured–type known as "red burley," which seems to have been used primarily in plug tobacco products. It has since faded to near nonexistence. A related strain that arose from a quite unintentional bit of plant breeding led to the almost complete decline of red burley in favor of a new "white" strain that appeared in Brown County, Ohio, in 1864.

Remember that at this time, chewing products dominated domestic consumption, with plug tobacco a popular consumer choice. Large-scale cigarette production was years in the future, but the new burley strain quickly

A costumed reenactor at Jamestown Settlement Park demonstrates how the colonists would have scouted for suckers and insect pests. *Photo by Chris Bickers.*

took a place in the manufacture of chewing production. Indeed, the initial appeal of white burley to manufacturers may have been aesthetic—light-colored leaves taken from it could be used to wrap plug products that otherwise probably contained very dark leaf.

Burley gained in popularity almost immediately, and its growth spread throughout Kentucky and down to Tennessee and then into West Virginia, Virginia and North Carolina and points farther away. Its position has never slackened.

Prior to 1924, burley production in Tennessee was largely confined to the eastern part of the state, and the total acreage for the state that year was 31,500 acres. Burley farmers in 1924 harvested just over twenty-seven million pounds. Production of burley has increased considerably since that time.

Smokers have found that the taste of cigarettes improves considerably with the addition of burley tobacco. Traditionally, about one-third of the tobacco in American-blend cigarettes is burley. The leaf is also used in domestic pipe and chewing tobaccos, and a little goes into some varieties of snuff.

THE PORT OF NEW ORLEANS

We might say that tobacco first gained its status as a commercial crop in Tennessee at about the time that the American Revolution ended. Most of the tobacco then was used purely for domestic purposes because it was extremely difficult to export mountain tobacco to major ports in the country. It could have been shipped to New Orleans via the Mississippi River, but New Orleans was controlled by the Spanish, who did not allow the tobacco to enter that port. "Roading" the hogsheads of tobacco over the Appalachians was virtually impossible.

Nevertheless, in 1787, an American general named James Wilkinson loaded two flatboats in the vicinity of Frankfort, Kentucky, with many consumer items, including bacon, flour and a good quantity of tobacco valued at two dollars per one hundred pounds.

Wilkinson intended his shipment for New Orleans, but he was well aware that the authorities would seize his two flatboats when they reached the Natchez area. This happened, but the confiscated cargo was released, and Wilkinson was asked to meet with Don Esteban Miró, then governor of Louisiana. Good relations were established between these two men, and thus the "Spanish intrigue," which has since puzzled historians, had its start.

Many believed that Wilkinson, a famous American general who served with Benedict Arnold in the Quebec campaign, was involved in a plot to separate the western territories from the United States and place them under the protection of Spain. Whether or not this was true, when Wilkinson returned to Frankfort in February 1788, New Orleans was opened to American trade. The Spanish authorities, already large buyers of Mississippi and Louisiana tobacco, now offered to buy the commodity from both Kentucky and Tennessee.

The Mississippi Opens to Tobacco

In December 1788, a royal order issued in Seville permitted Americans to enter goods at Mississippi River ports on payment of the Spanish entry duty. Initially, Wilkinson was shocked at hearing of the Spanish order. He had planned to monopolize trade with the Spanish at New Orleans. He was now competing with the rest of the country. Though the river was open to those who dared risk its passage, Wilkinson had the advantage of precedence, the right political connections and a developing organization.

All shipments were at the owners' risk—and the risks were significant. Apart from the physical hazards of river traffic that caused boats to capsize, sink or run aground, there were river pirates and Indians to contend with.

For a while, too, outlaws and white renegades infested the long route. A call for help, if answered, frequently resulted in the seizure of a boat and the massacre of its crew.

Much of the tobacco used during this period was manufactured at home in the form of "twists" for chewing and cigars. Practically all country stores sold "sticks" of twists, which were commonly used by the average working man. The elite used only James River tobacco and smoked Spanish cigars.

By the turn of the nineteenth century, tobacco figured more profitably in proportion to total income to the farmers of the Cumberland Valley. One of the first warehouses in the area was built in Pulaski County, Kentucky, on the Cumberland River and was known as Stigall's Warehouse. Crude as these tobacco warehouses were, they still sold a good deal of tobacco down the Mississippi. Stigall's reported, on the average, annual inspection of 217 hogsheads, and nearby Montgomery Warehouse reported inspection of 294. Each hogshead weighed around one thousand pounds, proving the inspection totals to be far from insignificant.

Wilkinson's boast that he had opened the Mississippi was justified. Customs records at New Orleans for 1790 showed that more than a quarter of a million pounds of tobacco had been registered in that port alone. An incalculable amount was smuggled in or went to sea without benefit of customs permits.

Western tobacco shipments increased to the point where much more of it was flowing down the river than could be sold. In 1790, Spanish authorities were forced to limit the amount of tobacco traded at New Orleans and set the maximum intake at forty thousand pounds annually. In late 1791, Wilkinson, "disgusted by disappointment and misfortunes, the effect of my ignorance of commerce," abandoned his export trade and reentered the United States Army.

In 1802, Spain withdrew the right of deposit in New Orleans from Americans. But Napoleon, who had purchased the entire Louisiana Territory from Spain, sold it to the United States in April 1803 for $11,250,000. The tobacco trade in Tennessee and its neighbors was stepped up again. An American merchant marine took shape, and western tobacco began competing in markets all over the world.

But international troubles were already brewing. President Jefferson, in an attempt to deplete French and British supplies of American tobacco, cotton and other commodities, declared an embargo on these products in 1807, and instead of being traded overseas, the tobacco rotted at the wharves, never to be sold. Meanwhile, the British navy was impressing American seamen, and both Great Britain and France were blockading American ports. American neutrality was violated as tobacco and other commodities were seized at sea. In 1808, the president, after much controversy, ended the embargo while his countrymen jeered that "embargo" spelled backwards read: "O grab me."

The troubles with England led to the War of 1812. The Capitol in Washington was burned to the ground, but in the end, the British were defeated, thanks to a considerable degree to the role the Long Rifles of Kentucky and Tennessee played, especially at the Battle of New Orleans in January 1815. Even though this famous encounter took place two weeks after the signing of the peace treaty at Ghent, their victory, under the leadership of Andrew Jackson, saved the entire Mississippi Valley from invasion.

By 1815, with the seas cleared and open to American shipping, leaf exports snapped back to ninety million pounds annually from well below sixty million during the British embargo.

In 1816, tobacco production around the Nashville-Clarksville area was estimated at ten thousand hogsheads. With tobacco as a well-established staple crop, the business of shipping leaf down the Mississippi to New Orleans was becoming more lucrative with each passing day. The postwar era was truly that of good feeling. Commerce and trade flourished as it never had before.

In 1830, the western tobacco fields of Kentucky and Tennessee were turning out one-third of the nation's crop. The Tennessee tobacco industry, for the first time, was making the transition from a supplier of tobacco for export and home use to a supplier of raw material for domestic manufacture. During that same year, one-fifth of the crop was not sent out of the country. It stayed in the United States for domestic manufacture, an ever-growing industry. Twenty-one Tennessee counties were each producing more than one million pounds of tobacco, and of these, eight produced almost two million pounds. Both Clarksville and Springfield were becoming popular as the largest dark-fired tobacco markets in the world, as more farmers were marketing their leaf on "home ground" and fewer were "prizing" it for shipment to New Orleans.

In 1834, the East Tennessee and Georgia Railroad was completed to Knoxville, supplying, for the first time, rail transport to the Atlantic ports and opening middle Tennessee to more trade.

Upon completion of new railroad systems and better river travel, including the steamboat, commerce from Tennessee flowed south down the Mississippi and as far east as New York. Tennessee corn, potatoes, whiskey, bacon, cider, apples, hemp, tobacco, beef, butter, cheese, beeswax, lard, feathers and cornmeal went to the markets of northern Alabama and the lower Mississippi. Although not luxurious, life for many Tennessee farmers was quite comfortable.

The increased production of cotton and wheat in Tennessee inhibited the growth of tobacco for a while. Shortly before the Civil War, Tennessee wheat commanded a premium price on the New York market. But according to the census of 1840, Tennessee ranked third in tobacco production behind Virginia and Kentucky. In that year, it produced 29,550,432 pounds. The total amount produced in the country that year came to more than 200 million pounds.

The Mexican War of 1846 caused a temporary reduction in the production of American tobacco, and at the dawn of the Civil War, Tennessee tobacco production was still limited to the northwestern and north-central parts of the state. Burley made up a small part of it. Tennessee farmers were still producing dark tobacco, which was especially in great demand on foreign markets. In 1859, Virginia still led the country in total tobacco production, but Kentucky followed a close second. Tennessee ranked third again, recording almost 43.5 million pounds.

In 1860, nine-tenths of all the tobacco grown in the United States came from slave states. Virginia, North Carolina, Kentucky and Tennessee accounted for about four-fifths of the nation's total. The South was also a great tobacco-manufacturing area. Just before the war, other than New York, the principal manufacturing centers of tobacco were Richmond, Petersburg, Lynchburg and Danville, Virginia; Clarksville, Tennessee; Henderson, Kentucky; Fayette and St. Louis, Missouri; and Milton, North Carolina.

The war proved disastrous to the tobacco industry of the South. For all intents and purposes, it virtually ceased to function, and it was not until the Reconstruction period that tobacco production and manufacture began to rebound.

The dark-fired areas prospered again, and with the development of burley, tobacco production started to spread throughout the state. Tobacco factories in the state became almost as numerous as textile factories and grain mills. Licorice and sugar were imported in large amounts for use in special chewing tobaccos. Before the end of the nineteenth century, a variety of plugs with enticing brand names such as "U Jo's, Five-Cent Pocket Piece," "Peach and Honey," "Old Time," "The Old Tennessee Twist," "Half Bushel," "Select Brazil Smoking" and "All Southerners" represented one of the major stable sources of income for almost any country store.

Tobacco products did not escape the attention of the revenue collectors, even one hundred years ago. In 1874, while writing a treatise on Tennessee's resources, state commissioner of agriculture Joseph Killebrew said, "We

Planting with a peg. By 1870, the peg made transplanting easier. In this demonstration at the Duke Homestead Historical Site in Durham, North Carolina, one costumed volunteer carries plants in a basket while another pegs and drops plants, followed by another who applies water from a gourd. *Photo courtesy of Duke Homestead Historical Site.*

A homemade transplanting peg. *Photo by Chris Bickers.*

have dwelt long on tobacco because it is the only great product of the state that is subject to a burdensome tax, and every effort of our people should be made to reduce or lighten the load upon their industry. In 1875, the Tennessee tobacco crop came to 35 million pounds."

The next year, Commissioner Killebrew stressed in a letter to the governor:

> *Tobacco, unlike cotton, does not interfere in any considerable degree with the cultivation of the grasses or bread grains, because the quality of tobacco planted is not limited, as cotton, by the number of acres which can be plowed, but by the ability to worm, sucker and house the crop. Consequently the saving in the amount of plowing, as compared with cotton, is so great that a tobacco planter may always make abundant supplies of corn, hay, wheat and other crops…The tobacco crop is, therefore, in a degree an extra crop, which, while it supplies the planter with ready money, does not interfere with his raising abundant supplies* [of other crops].

THE HILL COUNTRY'S FORGOTTEN TOBACCO TYPE

Burley wasn't the only tobacco that was grown commercially in Tennessee, southwest Virginia and western North Carolina. "Not many people know that flue-cured tobacco was grown in Greene County at one time," says Arthur Ricker of Greeneville, Tennessee. "I remember the old log barns and the furnaces on the outside that they used to heat the barns. But the farmers had a lot of problems with curing. If it cured too fast, it caused the leaf to be green. Later on, farmers here went to burley, and it worked better."

But before that, tobacco manufacturers were looking for new sources of flue-cured—or bright leaf. As a result, the agriculture of the mountains enjoyed a brief period of prosperity connected with the flourishing flue-cured market.

It had been introduced at least by 1868 and possibly earlier. Ten years later, the type had become a significant part of the agricultural economy. Buncombe County (county seat Asheville), North Carolina; the county just north of it, Madison County (Marshall), North Carolina; and the county just north of Madison, Greene County (Greeneville), Tennessee, all played particularly strong roles. Asheville and Greeneville developed markets that were at one time quite vigorous.

It was grown extensively in Virginia, as well. "Before burley was introduced in southwest Virginia, a very limited amount of flue-cured tobacco was grown in Washington County," says Jim Ed Cozart of Abingdon, Virginia. "It was on the north branch of the Holston River and some other areas. Some of those log buildings with their heating units outside still stand."

Flue-curing technology and bright tobacco varieties were adopted in the mountains nearly simultaneously with their diffusion in the Piedmont of Virginia and North Carolina and the coastal plain of the Carolinas and Georgia, says Katie Algeo, geographer at Western Kentucky University. "This adoption…by large numbers of farmers in the 1870s and 1880s [in areas where burley is now grown] was a response to increased market access and the diffusion of innovations in tobacco culture."

Peak production ran roughly from 1878 to 1890, but even then it was subject to highs and lows. For instance, in Madison County—nestled right on the border with Tennessee in the high mountains of the Blue Ridge—farmers took to flue-cured with abandon. They produced 807,000 pounds in 1879 at the beginning of the boom and then 2.2 million pounds ten years later. But starting in 1890, the bubble seemed to have burst, and by 1899, Madison Countians produced only 603,000 pounds.

What happened? These were the years of the Tobacco Trust, and trust buyers may simply have lost interest in mountain flue-cured. But historian Nannie May Tilley thinks competition from better-suited production areas might be the real reason. "Increase in cigarette consumption [at that time] doubtless contributed to abandonment of Bright Tobacco in the mountain area, since a more suitable type [for cigarettes] could be produced in greater quantity in the coastal plain," says Tilley. Leaf dealer William E. Dibrell described the mountain production as "showy, leafy, silky and free of the disease but also rather 'greenish always, with a decidedly unripe and ever rank flavor.'" In the final analysis, Tilley concludes, "Soil and climate prohibited cultivation of a mild type in the mountain area." A few holdouts continued flue-cured production on and off, but it seems to have disappeared by 1920. But the effort lived on in another sense: farmers and farms that had been involved in flue-cured production tended to be the ones to adopt burley production later.

Tennessee Burley Turns from Red to White

Meanwhile, a new type of tobacco was making its presence felt. It had mutated from an existing type. Here is how A.F. Ellis, a neighbor of George Webb, described that mutation in an article written in 1875:

White Burley first made its appearance in the year 1864, near the village of Higginsport, Brown Co., Ohio [forty miles south of Cincinnati]. *In the spring of that year one George Webb procured from G.W. Barkley, of Bracken County, Ky.* [just across the Ohio River from Higginsport], *a small portion of tobacco seed of the kind then known as Little Burley. He sowed a part of this seed and grew a bed of fine-looking plants, but when ready to transplant found among them a few of a peculiar white or yellow color and, supposing them to be diseased or dwarfed plants, pulled them up and threw them away.*

The next year, being scarce of seed, he sowed the remainder of this old seed and again found a portion of the same kind of plants that he had thrown away the year previous. This excited the curiosity of Mr. Webb and others, whose attention had been called to these strange-looking plants, and they were induced to transplant them, raising in all about 1,000 plants, which proved to be healthy and thrifty, and when fully ripe were almost of a cream color, making a great contrast with other tobacco. The result of this experience created quite a sensation throughout the neighborhood and many growers came from every direction to see what they called a freak of nature. The tobacco cured a bright yellow or cream color, but was adjudged bitter to the taste. Some concluded that although the tobacco colored well and produced the pounds, on account of its bitter taste it would not be safe to plant any large portion of the next crop of this kind of tobacco, although considerable seed had been saved. The plant beds that were sown of this seed in the year 1866 were found to contain a much larger portion of white plants than green ones, and a sufficient quantity were transplanted to produce 20,000 pounds of cured tobacco.

Two hogsheads of this production were shipped to the Cincinnati market and sold at a high price. The purchaser shipped the same to the St. Louis Fair of 1867 and, after being awarded the first and second premiums for cutting leaf, sold it for 58 per hundred. The remainder of this kind of tobacco… entered at the Cincinnati Annual Tobacco Fair of the same year to compete for the best 10 hogsheads of any class, and awarded the third premium, and was afterwards sold for 34 per hundred. The record thus made at the several tobacco fairs of 1867 induced many of the enterprising planters of Brown County, Ohio, and Bracken County, Ky., to plant largely of this kind of tobacco, and its culture has been gradually increasing throughout the entire district used for producing cutting tobacco until the present time, when it would be difficult to find any person in this large tobacco region so ignorant of his pecuniary interest as to plant any other kind.

THE NEW TYPE SPREADS

After white burley had been derived from red burley, production seeped south from Ohio, through Kentucky and down into Tennessee—especially in the eastern portion of the state.

But agriculture commissioner Killebrew, by the way, had the foresight to predict that of the divisions of the state, central Tennessee would eventually prove to be best suited for white burley production. "The central basin of Tennessee, of which Nashville is the center, by reason of its blue limestone soils, which have the same geological and lithological character as those in White Burley district of Kentucky, presents the most promising field for the extension of the culture of this most desirable product," he wrote in 1897. "Some is already grown in Trousdale, Wilson, Smith, and a part of Mason [*sic*] in the upper Cumberland river tobacco district, in Tennessee and in several of the counties in the same tobacco district in Kentucky."

THE COMING OF CAMELS

Much of the spread can be attributed to the phenomenal market success of a new brand of cigarette from R.J. Reynolds Tobacco.

After the breakup of the tobacco monopoly, Richard Joshua Reynolds's company was left with no cigarette brands to produce, and Reynolds wanted badly to change that situation. He and staff members began to look for a cigarette blend that would be economical in production cost but would also have an appealing taste that could capture a significant share of the market. They looked at the cigarette brands that were popular at the time in the United States and saw that those whose blends contained mostly or entirely oriental tobacco—the aromatic leaf grown in Greece, Bulgaria and Turkey—commanded the largest share of the market. Other popular brands had blends made up entirely of flue-cured Virginia, which was and still is the type grown in the Winston-Salem area. And some were a mix of oriental and flue-cured. These latter types seem to have formed the takeoff point for Reynolds and his team. They settled on a blend that was based on about half flue-cured. It accounted for what one might think of as the "tobacco-y" flavor of a cigarette. He needed to include at least some oriental, which brings a spicy flavor and aromatic character to a cigarette. But oriental was expensive in the early part of the twentieth century since it had to be imported from overseas. So Reynolds turned to the less-expensive domestic burley type, which was available from Kentucky and nearby states.

Perhaps drawing on his successful development a few years earlier of the innovative pipe blend Prince Albert, Reynolds recognized burley's key characteristic: its outstanding capacity to absorb flavoring. By some estimates, burley could take in 25 percent of its own weight in flavorings, compared to less than 10 percent for flue-cured Virginia. That characteristic made it possible for Reynolds to use burley that was flavored—or "cased," as it was called then—to substitute flavor elements for those that would be lost if he cut back on oriental. And that is what he did. Instead of 50 percent Virginia and 50 percent oriental, his blend ended up containing around 55 percent Virginia, around 10 to 15 percent oriental and the remaining 30 to 35 percent burley (percentages are approximate). He gave the brand he made with this blend the name Camel, and on its pack he said it was made with Turkish and domestic tobaccos, perhaps to allay any consumer fears that oriental had been eliminated altogether. It was an instant success. The public bought 425 million Camel cigarettes that first year, and four years later, Camel was the most popular cigarette in the United States. By 1925, more than half of the cigarettes smoked in the United States were Camels, and the glory years for American burley were just beginning.

Meanwhile, the expanding burley crops brought improving prices, reaching forty cents a pound by 1916. In 1921, the East Tennessee Tobacco Association and the state Department of Agriculture launched a campaign that led to burley planting in more than twenty counties. They produced a total crop of more than eighteen million pounds. A market was opened in Knoxville around 1923, and burley planting spread throughout the middle part of the state. The tobacco economy was hurt, but only temporarily, by the post–World War I deflation.

Why Early Growers "Split" the Stalk

According to research studies on the curing of leaf tobacco by Wightman Wells Garner, Charles Walter Bacon and Charles Lon Foubert (1914):

In some tobacco districts the stalk is split longitudinally from the top down the greater part of its length at the time the plant is harvested. Under these conditions the stalk cannot remain alive in the barn as long as when it is merely severed from the rootstock.

A special experiment was carried out to secure information on this point. Two similar lots of 10 plants each were selected and the stalks of one lot were split in the manner followed by growers. Each alternate leaf was picked from the plants in both lots and the two lots of leaves thus obtained were cured separately. The leaves remaining on the stalks were cured under the same conditions as the primed leaves. When the curing was complete the dry weights were obtained as in the preceding experiments. At that time the unsplit stalks were still green while the split stalks had largely dried out… Our conclusion: When the stalk is split in harvesting, the loss in weight in curing is less than when the stalk is not split.

Throughout the 1900s, tobacco production in Tennessee steadily increased. Although the total acreage harvested has been a good deal more

An early method of harvesting tobacco was to split the stalks in half from the top to near the ground surface with a sharp knife like this and then hang them over a stick. *Photo by Chris Bickers.*

This farmer in southern Virginia prefers a light tobacco knife with a sharp edge on the bottom of the head to cut both types. *Photo by Chris Bickers.*

in the past than it is now, technology and science have afforded the modern tobacco farmer an opportunity to produce a lot more tobacco per acre than his historical counterparts.

In 1920, for example, the average yield of tobacco per acre in Tennessee was 760 pounds. In the latest year of record, 2013, Tennessee burley farmers produced an average of 2,238 pounds per acre.

Tobacco production has come a long way in Tennessee since the pioneer days. The science of tobacco farming and marketing has evolved more and more into a united effort to produce a more refined crop much more efficiently.

2

VETERAN GROWERS REMEMBER BURLEY IN THE OLD DAYS

Bob Shipley, Farmer, Vilas, North Carolina

For about eighty-five years, burley has been a major cash crop and farm income source in the mountains of North Carolina. But it wasn't always. The big change in tobacco here in the mountains came when the federal quota program went into effect. We saw an increase in price so that farmers who grew it had some money left over after paying their expenses of growing tobacco. It was a good change. From that time, tobacco paid taxes and supported the schools and churches.

When burley first came along, it was a relatively new product. We didn't get into the tobacco business significantly till on up in the '30s. The Extension Service promoted it. It was an additional source of income. The farmers who didn't have allotments were anxious to get them and have them attached to their property. It wasn't too easy to come by allotments.

Allotments were originally issued based on your history of growing tobacco. If you hadn't grown burley before the program, you could grow some [outside the program] and get an allotment that way. Before allotments, the tobacco prices were so low [that] they only provided a little cash income, not much. At ten cents a pound, there was not much money to be made in tobacco. Prices improved markedly when the program went into effect. There was a stable year or two, but then for some reason, the price declined in 1939, and the growers voted the program out. But then things really went

Bob Shipley walks in his burley field near Vilas, North Carolina. *Photo by Chris Bickers.*

bad, and the growers were very quick to seek permission to vote it back in. It was never close to being voted out again after that.

I think we started in the program in 1937, so we had about sixty-five years of regulation. It ended in 2004, and there were a lot of complaints at the end. But as far as I am concerned, it was one of the most successful programs that [the] USDA ever sponsored. A very significant step in the program came when they converted from control of burley tobacco by way of acreage planted to control by poundage marketed in 1971. It was a major improvement in the program, I thought. But it took a little while to catch on.

I got into tobacco after my uncle gave me a farm in 1929. I hadn't worked in tobacco myself before that. I started growing it on my farm in 1931 with a farmer [who] was interested in sharecropping tobacco on my farm that year. I brought him in, and we had close to an acre that year. I rented it out to him on a share basis. I furnished the land, fertilizer and seed, while the grower furnished all the labor. He and his family stayed four years. I dealt with different farmers, and with their help, I grew burley on my farm until the last year of the program, 2004.

Marketing in this area wasn't easy at first. We took our tobacco to Johnson City, Tennessee [about fifty miles west], to market it. The first warehouse in Boone, the seat of Watauga County, wasn't built until 1940.

Here is the reason I decided to grow tobacco: Even with the lack of a local market, it was the most dependable crop you could produce here. We didn't have any other dependable cash crop in this area. That was the big reason that burley spread in the mountains.

Here is an example. In 1973, my friend Bill Harmon, who grew burley in the Sugar Grove community right by the Watauga River, told me that he made enough money from one acre of burley to buy a 3600 Ford tractor. Try buying a tractor of that size today with the profits of one acre of anything! He told me he made about $6,000, and there was a little left after he bought the tractor [for more details, see the interview with Bill Harmon]. That is why growers in this area were so interested in burley.

One disadvantage we face in growing burley in the mountains at a high elevation is the weather we have. Some

Top: Bob Shipley and Ernest Harmon survey Harmon's burley in the high mountains of Ashe County, North Carolina. *Photo by Chris Bickers.*

Right: Bob Shipley and Joe McNeil review the progress of the Watauga County, North Carolina tobacco crop in 2011. *Photo by Chris Bickers.*

A word from the commissioner. Bob Shipley enjoyed a good talk with North Carolina commissioner of agriculture Steve Troxler at the 2012 North Carolina State Fair. *Photo by Chris Bickers.*

years, we have an early frost that causes losses. Serious frost damage and reduced maturity in the cured leaf may result. At the end of the season, we may have to cut a little on the green side in order to beat the weather conditions. Farmers are trying to avoid this problem by using varieties that mature a little sooner. It is sort of an iffy situation that we have to deal with because we grow burley at a higher elevation than any other producing area.

GEORGE MARKS, FARMER, CLARKSVILLE, TENNESSEE

This area traditionally produced dark tobacco, but we didn't start producing burley. The first burley market in these parts was here in Clarksville in 1949. At that time, the price of dark tobacco was pretty dismal. The war had wrecked demand, most of which was in Europe. I don't know what they used it for, but the Europeans were our main customers. There wasn't much of a domestic market. So burley came here at a good time. So many farmers were looking for an alternative to dark tobacco, and a lot took up burley then. If you wanted to make [up] for the loss of dark demand or to expand, it was the only way.

Farmers here didn't start growing burley here [in north-central Tennessee] until after World War II, when the price of the dark fire-cured tobacco that was traditionally grown here fell very low. Many built new barns for burley, but some opened up dark barns and used them to cure burley in. Also, at

Right: George Marks grows burley and fire-cured near Clarksville, Tennessee. *Photo by Chris Bickers.*

Below: Two modern curing barns on the farm of George Marks of Clarksville, Tennessee. *Photo by Chris Bickers.*

that time, it hadn't been that long since the transition from mules to tractors, and a lot of old stables were left that could be converted into burley barns. Dark barns are much tighter than burley barns because they have to hold smoke. Burley barns have to be more open to air movement.

The price differential lasted till the '60s, when smokeless [products] became more popular. Now we have the opposite situation as when I first started. Dark brings much more than burley. There is not the interest in burley that there should be. I think it would take another dime per pound…to get the burley grown that we need.

The old splitting method of harvesting tobacco prevailed for a long time in this area for both types. You took a small knife and pushed it down into the butt end of the stalk about two-thirds of the way. Then you cut it off close to the ground with the same knife and laid it on the ground to wilt. That was the advantage—when it

Top: One timesaving advance in burley production: production of plants in trays floating in water in a plastic-covered greenhouse. The labor saving is enormous. *Photo by Chris Bickers.*

Left: George Marks re-sets a stick that has fallen over in his field. If conditions permit a full wilt, the stalks are much lighter and more maneuverable.

A field of tobacco wilts after cutting and spearing in one of George Marks's fields near the Cumberland River. *Photo by Chris Bickers.*

was split, it would wilt a lot quicker. That is still a problem with dark; it is so brittle that you have to let it wilt for a while to avoid breakage. But if it is hot, the leaf sunburns if you leave it out too long. Also, you didn't have to spike it. You could just hold the stick in one hand and hang the stalks over it with the other. Still, cutting and spiking required less labor and didn't require as much skilled labor. There weren't many men who had the skills needed to split tobacco. I don't know of anyone who still splits.

JOHNNY SHIPLEY, FARMER, CHUCKEY, TENNESSEE

I was born into tobacco growing. My daddy was a farmer. His family raised tobacco back when he was a boy. I guess this is how I got my start in tobacco, by growing up with it all my life. But when I graduated from college, I went into accounting for a while.

The late Johnny Shipley of Chuckey, Tennessee, said, "Without burley, it would have been hard to keep the farm in the family. It was the only big cash crop we had." *Photo by Chris Bickers.*

I remember working in tobacco from age five. I always had a job. I started out dropping plants. I had to pull the plants out of the bed. You always wanted [to do it] on a wet day so you could peg it out. There was no such thing as a setter, except for the old hand setter. You put the water in, threw the plant in the setter and then tripped it.

You would dig it out with a piece of wood that had a handle on it. You would try to find a crooked piece of wood and carve it so it was about ten inches long, It would have a curved handle, and it was sharpened, so it would penetrate the ground easily, stick a plant in, take the peg and knead the dirt around the roots.

We raised everything we needed in those days. On our farm, we grew bell peppers, watermelons and cantaloupes. Tobacco was the cash crop.

In the old days, all the neighbors helped when it was time to harvest. Several ladies would come in and make lunch. Everybody helped everybody then. We would have beans, potatoes, corn and some kind of meat—ham or roast. We had very little milk because there was no refrigeration then. We would cut and hang in late November or December. Now, all that is done primarily with Mexican labor.

We didn't need as many people to strip and grade the crop as we did to harvest. One man can throw it out of the barn. Usually, the families could do the rest of the work, so not too much outside help was needed for grading.

You would try to make a warm corner in the barn to serve as a grading room. It needed to be well insulated, and it usually had a small heater of some kind. You might put a little water on heat for humidity. That would help make the leaf pliable.

For children, it was always something to do when you got home from school when I was growing up. Now I hire someone else to do it.

After working as an accountant for several years, I started growing tobacco again. I also started a plant business. They fit together pretty well. Tobacco gives my employees something to do in the winter months.

I do it because I enjoy it. But it is not that profitable because of the high cost of production. I will miss tobacco when I stop. Without burley, it would have been hard to keep the farm in the family. It was the only big cash crop we had. It was your Christmas money, it was your back to school money, it was shoe and clothing money.

Note: Johnny Shipley passed away in August 2012.

David Miller, Farmer, Abingdon, Virginia

My grandfather started growing burley back in 1913, and 2013 was our one-hundredth year. His name was Benjamin Miller Sr. He hadn't grown any other tobacco before burley, as far as I know. His motivation was that he was looking for a cash crop, which he needed

David Miller of Abingdon, Virginia, celebrated the centennial year of his tobacco farm in 2013. *Photo by Chris Bickers.*

There has often been a shortage of curing space. This old dairy building on the Miller farm has frequently been dragooned into duty to cure burley. *Photo by Chris Bickers.*

A healthy plant is terrifically valuable for a modern burley grower. *Photo by Chris Bickers.*

Miller has concentrated on efficiently producing plants in the greenhouse so that now, selling plants to other farmers is a profitable sideline. *Photo by Chris Bickers.*

badly. At that time, he was sharecropping in the north part of Washington County. He moved to this farm (five miles east of Abingdon) and started planting burley here in 1941. The soil here in the Appalachian ridges and valleys is loamy and is good for burley. I don't know how much my grandfather grew at his first farm, but once he moved here, three acres was a normal crop. He was also a dairy farmer.

He built traditional wooden tier barns to cure his tobacco, none more than three tiers high. We still use most of them. When we have had to build more barn space, it has been outdoor curing structures.

My father, Benjamin Miller Jr., grew tobacco also, and now I am doing it.

If I were going to point to the biggest difference between how my grandfather grew tobacco and the way I do it now, it is the way we produce plants. My grandfather would have seeded outdoor beds and grown them under cheesecloth. I produce plants in two thirty- by ninety-six-foot greenhouses. I grow them for myself and also sell quite a few. I also sell greenhouse vegetable plants. It has been a learning process. The most important practice in producing greenhouse transplants is frequent inspection. You've got to practically live with them. We inspect ours five to ten times a day during the season. In 2012, that went from March, when we started seeding, to May 5, when planting started.

Another very important part of greenhouse plant production is clipping. That is something my grandfather probably never thought about. We clip ours usually three to five times each season. My general rule is that if I have to clip my plants more than four times, I may have seeded too early.

We have gone to one of Grandfather's practices that we had gotten away from. In recent years, we have cut our tobacco when we harvested it and put it in the barn the same day. But we can't hardly do that now. We grow the new KT (Kentucky-Tennessee) varieties, and they are huge. So we try to leave our tobacco out for three to four days and wilt it to get the sunburn out. It reduces the weight. Otherwise, the labor can't get it in the barn.

We cure about like it's always been done. We hang all our tiers at one time. We stagger the tobacco in. Then it takes about six weeks to cure. We strip in the barn if it is warm. We go to a stripping room if it is cold. One person strips the whole stalk into three or four grades. That gives us one more chance to find bad leaves.

I don't know how confident I feel about the future of tobacco in this area because of the labor issue and because costs are so high and input costs absolutely are not decreasing.

The "lingo" used in tobacco changes from place to place. You don't have to go too far to find completely different language. Here, we spear. In Greeneville, they spud. Here, we hang. In Kentucky, they house. There are people who set tobacco and people who plant tobacco.

ERNEST HARMON, FARMER, ELK PARK, NORTH CAROLINA

I started helping my dad in tobacco at six. That was in 1938. His farm where I grew up is about three miles from here. I bought two small farms in 1954 and put them together and built a house there. Tobacco was the main crop. I grew it that first year and have been growing it myself ever since.

I farm in the mountains (near Beech Mountain). My fields are at an elevation of about 3,800 feet. They are mostly sloping. When we first started using tractors, we couldn't get them up some of the hills. I was very glad when four-wheel drive came along. It really gave us a big benefit on this land.

We have a lot of rain here in the mountains. You need some rain to get it in and out of case. If it is dry, your tobacco may cure out too quick. If you get enough rain, the tobacco gets the color that the buyers want. But you can

Right: Ernest Harmon raises burley at some of the highest elevations at which tobacco is grown in the United States. *Photo by Chris Bickers.*

Below: When the burley industry demanded that leaf be packed in bales, Harmon built his own bale boxes to save money and get them just the way he wanted them. *Photo by Chris Bickers.*

get too much rain. It might cause rot or barn scalding, where the leaf falls off or turns a real black color. You have some control. When it is too dry, you can open the doors, and when there is too much rain, you can close them up.

It takes about a month and a half to cure once it is in the barn. You have to get the stems to cure out as well as the leaf. In the old days, once it was cured and

Tobacco money paid for Ernest Harmon's house on his farm near Elk Park, North Carolina, he says. *Photo by Chris Bickers.*

Tobacco "knives" came in all shapes and sizes over the years on Harmon's farm. *Photo by Chris Bickers.*

stripped, we tied it in hands and put it in baskets. Now we press it into bales. It is a lot easier and saves a lot of labor.

The barns we use now are one to three tiers high. I used to have barns that were five tiers tall, but I don't climb as high as I used to. My barns have all been wood. Our tier poles were poplar or birch or any tree that was five or six inches wide. We cut them ourselves. The sticks were four feet long. We would put five or six stalks per stick.

I have grown burley every year since 1954. I will keep growing it as long as I can.

Benny Davis, Farmer, Surgoinsville, Tennessee

My family got into burley back in the '30s. I started in the early '50s when I was a kid. We had an old setter that was operated by hand. My first job was to carry water in four-pound buckets for the setters. That was hard work. Next, I went to dropping plants. Then we went mechanical with tractors. We got a one-row setter, and we would drop plants into it. Boy, we were in high cotton then! It really cut down on the labor needed to set tobacco.

We did cultivation and other field work with horses and mules for a long time. That is something I really miss, working with horses and mules. They were really something to watch. When I was young, we farmed with mules and horses both. We had no tractor. I always thought the mules were better for tobacco. The mules had smaller feet, and they wouldn't tramp the soil down as much as a horse would. Also, a horse will have a tendency to balk—to stand there and do nothing. I have never seen a mule balk.

Many of the old-timers claimed that using the tractor would pack the ground. Even after we had tractors, many didn't want to go over the field with the tractor after planting. They would use their draft animals instead for the rest of the work. One thing I liked about horses—a good workhorse, if it was broke right, you didn't need guides. You could just tell it "gee" and "haw." You could just speak to it, and the animal would understand.

You could use them in conditions where you might not be able to use a tractor. I remember about thirty years ago, long after we had let go of our draft animals, we had a patch of tobacco that we couldn't get into because it was wet. One of our neighbors had a pony that was broke to work. One of our boys went over and borrowed that little pony, hitched it to a four-foot plow and ran through

Benny Davis of Surgoinsville, Tennessee, remembers with fondness cultivating tobacco with horses and mules. *Photo by Chris Bickers.*

Davis shows a pair of draft horses at a field day in Hawkins County, Tennessee. *Photo by Chris Bickers.*

the tobacco [with a cultivator]. I was glad he was able to do it because that patch had a lot of morning glory, and he got rid of a lot of it. It wouldn't have been possible without the pony.

A demonstration of cultivation with horse-drawn equipment in Hawkins County, Tennessee. *Photo by Chris Bickers.*

The old conventional plant beds were used then. We cut brush, piled it and burned it in the late '80s. In the mid-'60s, we started using gas. We got the beds prepped and ready to sow; then we put plastic cover over the beds and gassed with methyl bromide. We would still have weeds but not nearly as bad. Pulling plants was hard. You would sit on a board and bend over the plants.

Plant production has been the biggest change in my lifetime. I went to greenhouses in the '90s. I wasn't real confident at first. I grew conventional beds as backup for the first two seasons. After that, we just grew in greenhouses for ourselves and we sold plants. We did that for about ten years. It got to be a good business. But after the buyout, we started losing customers. At our peak, we grew a million plants. We had twenty-two customers. Now I grow for one customer and myself. Everybody just quit after the buyout.

I have around ten acres of burley. My labor is a Mexican family who has worked for me since the '90s. It is a legal family. I do most of the tractor work, and I provide all expenses—plants, equipment, barns. He just has his labor. We split the profits fifty-fifty. When he is harvesting, he will have six people in the field, maybe eight. It is mostly his family, but sometimes he will recruit friends and relatives. If it wasn't for migrant workers, you couldn't raise tobacco any more. No one else wants to do it.

What gets me today is that the farmer is the only one in this business who has to buy retail and sell wholesale. It is hard for people to realize what a farmer has invested. It has got so that now there is no profit

One good thing about a workhorse that Benny Davis remembers: "If it was broke right, you didn't need guides. You could just tell it 'gee' and 'haw.'" *Photo by Chris Bickers.*

there. We have had buyout money, but most of it has gone elsewhere. Not tobacco. After the buyout, I hoped the companies would offer a high enough price that growers could stay in tobacco. If they cut the price, growers on leased land wouldn't grow it. And that is about what happened. Even the farmers who owned quota have been getting out. A lot hung on for the buyout. But they are getting out now. There will be a few diehards like me who will keep growing it.

JIM ED COZART, FARMER/WAREHOUSEMAN, ABINGDON, VIRGINIA

Many people don't know this, but before burley was introduced in southwest Virginia, a very limited amount of flue-cured tobacco was grown in Washington County. It was on the north branch of the Holston River and some other areas. Some of those log buildings with heating units outside still stand.

Following in the steps of his father (pictured on the wall), farmer Jim Ed Cozart of Abingdon, Virginia, spent much of his career as a tobacco warehouseman. *Photo by Chris Bickers.*

Burley was primarily a Kentucky crop then, though it actually originated in Brown County, Ohio. But it proved to be a good crop here in southwest Virginia. My father carried some burley seed here for American Tobacco when he came out here in 1919. The type of tobacco grown here at first was the type American Tobacco would use: thin, with high coloration. It was used in American blends, which were still new then.

Washington County is well suited to growing burley. We have many limestone soils, which are ideal for good burley. You need that limestone base for good burley. When it first came here, most of it was raised in the bottoms, and it still is. But we have a lot of hillsides in this area, and some was raised on the hills, too. You had to be careful with tobacco on the hillsides. You could get erosion problems. A lot of farmers had grass growing on the hills. Blacker soil usually was better for burley. You could get good growth in the sandy soil in the bottoms, but you didn't get the weight. Flat river bottoms weren't the best for tobacco either. The drainage is not as good. Tobacco needs good drainage away from the crop.

The city of Abingdon very definitely appreciated what tobacco meant for it. People paid their taxes with it, and it sent a lot of children to school. Debts were paid down. When the auctions were going on, there was extra money for the local economy. For many years, the city had a tobacco festival here that recognized the place it held. It moved around at first but ended up in a metal building by the fairgrounds. It featured competitions for tobacco stalks and for hands—the grading services would furnish a judge. There were also shows for cattle, sheep and goats; there was crocheting and basket weaving; and there was new machinery on display. It was a good occasion. They still do a similar event, but they don't call it the tobacco festival anymore.

We are still growing a little tobacco on a share crop basis. I had 140 acres at one time. I was down to 40 acres in 2011, but I still thought we were overextended, so we cut back to 22 acres in 2012 and made a good crop. I think we do a better job with less. I still have nine good tobacco barns. Most are the same size, 45 by 120 feet. We built some sheds. We made one change in our production in 2013, though I didn't want to do it. We contracted our plants out for the first time ever. I hate it that I have a greenhouse and am not growing plants in it, but I believe I am going to be better off this way. The year before last, we ran out of plants and had to buy more, and the ones I got weren't resistant to black shank, which I needed. I don't want that to happen again!

There was another change in 2013: Philip Morris had been handling our tobacco for some time, but they closed the plant here. We would have to carry it so far to another Philip Morris station—probably to Danville—that it wouldn't be worth the trip. So in 2013, we took it to [the Burley Stabilization Corporation buying station in] Greeneville, Tennessee.

Arthur Ricker, Farmer/Warehouseman, Greeneville, Tennessee

Not many people know that flue-cured tobacco was grown in Greeneville at one time. I remember the old log barns and the furnaces on the outside that they used to heat the barns. But the farmers had a lot of problems with curing. If it cured too fast, it caused the leaf to be green. Later on, farmers here went to burley, and it worked better.

I grew tobacco for seventy years, and the first crop I had was in 1940. I was eighteen. But then I was absent for five years because I went into the military.

When I was growing up on a tobacco farm, the boys did the hoe work, chopping out weeds. The older men did the cultivating. Back then, they just had a four-foot cultivating plow that was pulled by a horse. Later on,

Above: The Smoky Mountains rise in the distance as Arthur Ricker of Greeneville, Tennessee, walks through his family's tobacco crop.

Right: Rows of burley slope up an incline near Arthur Ricker's farm. *Photo by Chris Bickers.*

Arthur Ricker of Greeneville, Tennessee, grew burley over a seventy-year period. *Photo by Chris Bickers.*

I helped plow tobacco with a riding cultivator. Still later, we graduated to a tractor cultivator.

Back in those early years, they didn't have anything to plant with. There was no way to set tobacco except with a tobacco peg. I remember that was a bad job, bending over, setting tobacco all day. Finally, there came what was called a hand setter. That helped a lot. One man used the setter, and another dropped plants. Then they finally got a tractor setter. I started out with a one-row tractor setter, and later we got us a two-row setter, which took five people to operate.

We had a big change in plant production, too. Back in the old days, people grew their plants in beds, which were primarily in the woods. They would burn the soil to kill the weed seeds in the ground. That was a lot of work. In later years, we got hothouses. It was much easier to grow plants in them, and you could do it quicker.

When harvesting, they had knives and cut the stalks at the ground after they split it (from top to bottom). Later, they came up with a hatchet and used it and a spear to put the tobacco stalks on a stick. A lot of people were fearful that they would get injured by the sharp spear, and some did.

Later, after we cut the tobacco and stuck it in the field, we left it four to six days. But you had to watch out for sunburn because the tobacco would be green. If you had very heavy rains on it and left it out much later, the rain and the sun would discolor it. I never left it out seven days—but the longer you left it out in the field, the less weight you had to take to the barn, which helped with the labor.

Cutting and spearing was much better and easier than splitting. When you split down that stalk, you had to bend way over in order to cut the stalk off.

It was easier taking a hatchet and cutting it off like a tree. It was just easier doing it that way.

I am in my nineties now. I have been pretty active in burley till a few years ago. But now, my son and grandson tend my tobacco. There is not a great deal of profit in burley tobacco anymore. You have to farm on a large volume or you won't survive.

KENNETH REYNOLDS, FARMER, ABINGDON, VIRGINIA

Burley has been an important crop in southwestern Virginia all my life. I used burley money to send my daughter to college. Tobacco was a stabilizer for the economy. Abingdon was a center for tobacco marketing. At one time, it had eleven or twelve warehouses, and people brought their tobacco here from probably a forty- or fifty-mile radius. It had a tremendous impact here in our community. And farmers in Washington County did well with burley. There is something unique about the climate and soil here that produces something the market desires. Forty or fifty years ago, everybody made

Tobacco has been a stabilizer for the economy in and around Abingdon, Virginia, for most of Kenneth Reynolds's life. *Photo by Chris Bickers.*

Most of the burley on the Reynolds farm in most years was cured in multitier barns like this one. *Photo by Chris Bickers.*

money growing tobacco; it was just a matter of how much you got paid. Today, it's a matter of survival of the fittest. At one time, there were many growers here. Myself, I am a third-generation burley grower. My grandfather was the first burley grower in our family.

I didn't farm full-time at first. After college, I took a job with the Department of Agriculture, and I worked there during the day. But I was always here to help out with the tobacco. Later, I took early retirement because I needed to help my father with the farm. In 1991, I took over management of the farm. This was a dairy farm, but my dad grew some tobacco. I spent most of my growing up here. I still own the land. All these farms had tobacco. Farms here were usually thirty to seventy acres. We have cherty soil, but it had some clay. We produced essentially a red tobacco.

Growing tobacco was a lot different when we used methyl bromide to sterilize our soils. We would seed with our hands. Later, we used a seeder that we could push through the bed and spread the seed mixed with fertilizer. We covered it with cheesecloth. We would fix it in February. The plants would come up quickly. When the plants were ready, we pulled the cover back. We would take the big plants, then we might put the cheesecloth back so the small plants would have a few more days to grow. We used to have six or seven plant beds. We would put them in different locations. With a plant bed, you needed the sun to hit, so we had to find situations with sun. With our hills and valleys, that sometimes took some looking. We learned over the years what locations would grow plants the best.

Under cheesecloth, we had to monitor plants pretty close. If they got too big, we had to pull them and go right to the fields. You would kneel at the edges and reach in to get plants or put a board across the bed elevated by a piece of wood at each end and kneel on it. We would often load our plants on the tobacco baskets that we carried our leaf to the warehouse in. We would put the baskets on a trailer and keep it in the shade until we were ready to take them to the field. Plant beds took a lot of effort, but they worked. We got good plants most years.

There was a lot of pressure to do as well as you could on tobacco because there weren't many alternatives for generating cash on a farm in those days. Dairying was one. It was an excellent source of income here if you could do it. Many small farmers milked maybe twenty-five cows. Pet had a plant in Abingdon, and they would send trucks out into the country every day. There was another income source related to dairying. Sometimes the farmer would buy what we called "veal" calves from the dairies. It you could tend them till they reached two hundred pounds, a packing pant in Bristol would buy them. And a few farmers had sheep. They could sell the lambs at local livestock markets when they reached one hundred pounds. They had to generate as much additional income as they could beyond what they made from tobacco. But there weren't a lot of choices. There still aren't. Now we supplement tobacco income with feeder cattle and sheep.

When we learned that methyl bromide wasn't going to be available much longer, we had to switch to some other way of producing plants. So we changed from plants produced in beds to plants from a greenhouse. But we decided not to grow them ourselves—we bought them from other farmers. In fact, I never owned a greenhouse myself. It has never seemed economical to have a greenhouse when I can buy plants cheaper than I can produce them. We have five acres this year, same as last year, all grown on contract. We used to grow three times what we do now.

Most of the tobacco we grow has leaves growing close to the ground. But if you cut carefully, we can get all of them. We use light hatchets with very sharp blades to cut off the stalks close to the ground. Then we "spear" the stalks on a stick, which we hang from tier poles in the barn. In the old days, farmers harvested by cutting the stalk close to the ground with some kind of small knife after they had split it from top to nearly the bottom. Their thinking was that the split stalk would cure better, but it was a slow process. Cutting and spearing caught on quickly, and I think that is how everyone does it now.

Bill Harmon, Farmer, Sugar Grove, North Carolina

It seems to me that I have been involved in burley ever since I was born. That was in 1935 in Avery County. I lived there until I was twenty-six years old, when I bought this property [on the Watauga River near Boone].

There have been some big changes in growing tobacco while I was a farmer. Getting the tobacco set was one. When I was a child, we would lay rows out and mark them, fertilize them and make little hills. When the plant was ready, we would use the peg to make a hole and drop the plant in. That was hard work. Things worked better when we got the hand setter. It carried three gallons of water in a reservoir. You could "doodle" soil around the plants with it for a tighter set. When you planted with the peg, the plant did not set as well as it did with the hand setter. The peg was hard to use in hard ground, harder than the hand setter. I was still using the hand setter when I stopped growing.

When it came to the way of harvesting, there was a big change in my lifetime. My dad would build a set of sawhorses. Then he would split the stalk all the way down nearly to the base and hang it on the sawhorses. He thought it cured better that way. But I don't know anyone who still does that. Everyone uses a tobacco knife (a blade on a handle like a tomahawk sharp enough to cut in one swipe) and spears the stalks on a stick. They might hammer the stick into the ground with the knife, but I carried a maul and used it to drive the stick into the ground. If the dirt was soft enough, one hard lick would do it. In most cases when we harvested, we put six stalks on a stick. My tiers were framed four feet. I liked to leave it out over four days if possible. I set the stalks equally apart on the stick. That kept it straight on the trailer. I would put it even on the stick and leave it in that way. You'd get a rotten mess if it all was jammed together.

I was a carpenter, and I helped build several burley barns in the old days. The farmers back then would build them so they could draw a team of horses through them. They wanted plenty of sunlight, and they wanted the barn good and open so there would be plenty of air. Later, we learned to set tiers north and east so air went through easy. Barns were built in many locations. You could build a barn on a hill, but you had to watch out. I had a barn at five thousand feet in the Beech Mountain area, and I could get a good cure, but sometimes

Bill Harmon grew tobacco on the Watauga River near Boone, North Carolina, from the '60s until the buyout. *Photo by Chris Bickers.*

Two chestnut trees Harmon planted about ten years ago have flourished, despite the blight, in front of a barn that is well over one hundred years old. *Photo by Chris Bickers.*

before I could get it stripped, a damp spell and fog would come in. You might get mold or changed colors. That is why I think down in the bottoms is the best place to put a barn. You are less likely to get a fog there. In the '60s, you saw more modern barns built. You could drive through each section and back in with a tractor or truck. When we were using teams of horses, we had to go straight through. If I wanted to build a barn today, I would build it two tiers high so I could load it from a truck or tractor with one man handing up to a man standing on the first tier. With three tiers, you could get more tobacco in, but you would need more help to load. I would build each drive fourteen feet wide so I could back through with a truck or tractor.

My old barn was built sometime in the 1800s, and most of it was hemlock. When I got it, I tore out much of the insides and replaced it. I built new sheds on the big barn. It already had sheds, but they were rotting off. Hemlock

Top: Setting plants got easier when the hand transplanter was introduced. Bill Harmon holds an old one. *Photo by Chris Bickers.*

Left: When it was time to cut and spear, Bill Harmon liked to carry a wooden "maul" to drive the stick into the ground. *Photo by Chris Bickers.*

was the number one choice to build burley barns back then. But the hemlocks are about all dead. They have been killed by a little insect [hemlock woolly adelgid]. The American chestnut has also been cut way back by the chestnut blight. You don't see them in the woods here. But I have two chestnut trees in front of my old barn. I planted them eight years ago. A man had given me some seed from some trees in Kentucky that weren't killed by chestnut blight. They should be dead according to the way the blight usually kills chestnuts, but they are really doing good.

Tobacco was mighty good to us. It was the one crop you could just about be certain you would get rewarded on. In 1973, I made enough off an acre of tobacco to buy a tractor in one year. How much was that? I gave $3,600 for the tractor. I may have had a little left.

I did pretty well because, for many years, I averaged three thousand pounds to the acre. But because of diseases, I went down to two thousand pounds. I had to grow on the same land over and over again. It gets tired and it gets diseased, and it is not very good. When the buyout came along, I decided to get out. But that land has been setting there now for six or seven years. It's rested. If you planted burley there now, I reckon it would do real good. But I am not going to do it. I'm finished growing tobacco.

L.D. Simmons, Farmer, Johnson City, Tennessee

It's no surprise that burley is still grown here. The climate and humidity here and in western North Carolina is perfect to get the color and quality the burley buyers want. And burley is best grown on loamy soils like we have here.

Tobacco goes back nearly a hundred years in this area. A neighbor of ours grew tobacco in 1921 and 1922. Some of it was dark fire-cured, but a lot of it was burley. That got us to thinking about it. But we didn't start growing for a few more years. We had a tenant named Hill Stines, who said he wanted to grow burley, so Daddy agreed to build a barn for him. We began growing burley ourselves sometime after. Now, we haven't missed a year of tobacco in seventy years.

Like everywhere, you needed a good curing barn here. My dad had a barn he was proud of. It was five tiers high in the center and four tiers high on the sides. I remember that those top tiers cured beautifully. We would load the stalks on a wagon and drive it into the barn. There would be two to three men in the wagon passing the tobacco straight up above them.

Left: "It's no surprise that burley is still grown in east Tennessee," says L.D. Simmons of Johnson City. "The climate and humidity here and in western North Carolina is perfect." *Photo by Chris Bickers.*

Below: Simmons loads his conventional barn from a big wagon. *Photo by Chris Bickers.*

Some outdoor structures Simmons built help cure the crop if there is too much of it for the barns. *Photo by Chris Bickers.*

The man in the top tier had a tough job. If he wasn't careful, he might fall to the ground. I don't know that it is really that dangerous, but you have to be able to straddle four feet. I remember when Mexican workers first started coming up here, one of my migrant workers was so afraid of falling that he tied his shoelaces to the rails. He would have to untie them and tie them again when he moved, but he felt safer that way.

Five tiers in a barn were common. I remember another family had a barn that was seven tiers high, but they were short tiers. When it was full, the tobacco lapped on the tier below it.

My father built a couple of barns. Like most farmers, he added a shed later. I have one barn now. When I reached the point where I didn't have enough room to cure my tobacco, I put up some "racks" (outdoor curing structures). They have worked out.

Our farm grew corn for silage, wheat and hay before tobacco. It is good land. The corn grew fourteen feet tall. We had a dairy, and we used the silage and hay as feed. But we sold our dairy cows in 1962. We had beef cattle for thirty-six years.

I started helping my brother grade when I was ten or so. What I remember about it was that it was so cold, the coldest I'd ever been.

When I first started helping with transplanting, we were still using pegs. That was hard work. We got a setter, but we had a terrible time with the first one. The plants would stick. Then, in 1952, I bought a drag setter. It worked out good. After that, everyone wanted me to set for them—and not just tobacco, either. I also planted potatoes, beans and corn, raspberries and strawberries, even tomatoes. At first, we pulled it with a mule. That was hard—you had to train the mule to walk slow enough so we could put in the plants. Our next setter had a wheel on the front. We used it for I don't know how many years.

An acre and a half was what I grew under allotments. After the buyout, you were able to grow more. The most I grew was eight to ten acres. The price went down after the buyout, but it has made its way back up since then. Two years ago, we had twelve thousand pounds and sold for a price of $1.97 a pound. Last year (2013), we sold four thousand pounds for $2.05 a pound.

I have grown seventy consecutive crops here, but I almost missed one of the first ones. I was growing tobacco during World War II, and in 1945, I had to reset my tobacco on July 4. A few days later, I got my draft notice. I went into the navy, expecting to serve. I thought my crop would never get finished. But they dropped the bomb in August. They sent me home in September, and I finished my crop.

Joe McNeil, Farmer, Vilas, North Carolina

Tobacco has been very helpful for my family. I was born here in Watauga County near Boone, and I helped with the tobacco on our farm as far back as I can remember. My dad had started growing tobacco in the '20s, I think, and he sold it in Abingdon, Virginia.

"Life in the mountains would have been livable without tobacco," says Joe McNeil of Vilas, North Carolina. "But it wouldn't have had any of the frills." *Photo by Chris Bickers.*

Right: The tobacco rows stretch into the hills on Joe McNeil's farm in Vilas, not far from Boone, North Carolina. *Photo by Chris Bickers.*

Below: Harvest was about half complete on the day this picture was taken looking down on McNeil's burley field from a neighboring ridge. *Photo by Chris Bickers.*

McNeil has retired from farming but helps his neighbor with tobacco on this ridge. *Photo by Chris Bickers.*

In 1955, when I finished high school, my parents said I could raise tobacco here. "What you can make is yours, so you can send yourself to school," they told me. So it was that, from that time on, I raised tobacco for myself, until recently. I went into the service, then took aw year off. When I returned, I rented my aunt's farm and raised tobacco for her. About that time, my father decided to retire.

As a teenager, I liked to work. I was twelve or thirteen years old when I first worked tobacco. When I got to be sixteen, I got the opportunity to measure tobacco, too. I would measure each farm plot of tobacco. It was estimated decimally in links. I made more money measuring tobacco than I could make at a job working for Belks making four dollars a day. I could make as much as fifteen dollars a day measuring tobacco.

We were growing close to an acre most years, but as we got close to the buyout, I tried to grow more. When my wife and I got married in 1960, I didn't have anything. Dad gave me this land, and I built my house on it. The land served as collateral for borrowing money from FHA. I got $10,000 and built my house. We didn't have furniture except for a couch that my mother said we could have. So we owed for the car, and we owed for the house, but tobacco paid for our car and bought our furniture.

It paid for my children's education. One of my daughters, Mary, went to North Carolina State University. This was in the early '80s when tobacco was bringing $2 a pound. We worked the tobacco together with her, and in those years, we had good crops. I kept count of how much the costs of the inputs were. That was subtracted, and any profit went to her. It was enough money—perhaps $5,000—to pay her costs of going to college.

Her younger sister Melissa went to Appalachian State University. She had worked with us in tobacco until she was sixteen. Then she got a job in retail for about four years. But then she decided she wanted a share of the tobacco to help pay for college, and she came back and worked with us.

Since then, inputs have gone up and prices have come down. It is not as profitable now unless you have a large family that can do all the work. I can't really grow it myself anymore because I have had two hip surgeries. But I help my friend who grows burley across the ridge. I help on the land preparation, help him set, help him harvest and sometimes help him grade it. So I am still involved in tobacco.

When the girls were in college, we didn't have a tractor. It was all done by hand. Horses prepared the ground, and we planted with a hand transplanter. Our life would have been okay without tobacco, but it wouldn't have had any of the frills. It would have been just the basics.

ROBERT MILLER, TOBACCO BREEDER, GREENEVILLE, TENNESSEE

Burley, which originated in Brown County, Ohio, about the time of the Civil War, arrived years later in east Tennessee. Before that, I have been told that the tobacco grown here had been flue-cured. There was an attempt for several years at growing flue-cured, but it didn't last long. The conditions don't seem to have been well suited to it.

For burley, however, the region was and still is very well suited compared to other areas where burley is produced. East Tennessee has high humidity and lower temperatures and just a better environment for burley curing. Also, when the type moved in, there was ample availability of labor. That was important because burley required more labor than almost any other farm commodity we could produce here. That tended to mean that burley wound up on small farms with relatively small burley plantings. The farm families were generally large enough to provide the labor to get everything done. Once local farmers had the opportunity to grow burley, they found that they had the advantages of good curing conditions and labor availability. Since they couldn't really grow anything else as a cash crop here, it became a popular choice very quickly, especially in the area close to Greeneville. A farmer would often base his burley plantings on the amount of suitable land he had and on the number of family members he could bring to the field. Eventually, Greene County, Tennessee, had more burley than any other county in the United States, and that lasted for many years. It didn't change substantially until cross-county leasing went into effect. There has been more attrition since then. The end of the federal tobacco program was sort of the last straw. Now, there aren't nearly as many growers here as there used to be.

When I first came to work at the University of Tennessee Tobacco Experiment Station in 1982, I was surprised at how poor some of the tobacco crops were. Although many growers were producing excellent crops, several others were struggling. A lot of it had to do with varieties; most of the tobacco crops were being produced from older varieties that had limited disease resistance. To compound the problem, many of the smaller, part-time growers wouldn't know what variety they were growing—they simply used plants left over after their neighbors had finished transplanting. As a result, black shank and tobacco vein mottling virus were endemic in the region, greatly reducing yield potential. In dark tobacco–production areas of middle Tennessee and western Kentucky, several of the varieties in use when I first came here were essentially "landraces" [local varieties that have developed over time] that had little or no disease resistance. Farmers would save the seed of these varieties, and the identity was frequently not accurately assigned. A "variety" called Madole was the common dark tobacco variety at that time. But Madole seemed to include strains that were different from one another and might be distinct varieties. I tested them all and identified twelve different strains that could be called varieties themselves, but none had any disease resistance.

We have made a lot of progress in developing disease-resistant burley and dark tobacco varieties over the last thirty years. TN 86, the first burley tobacco variety we released, was the first variety that had resistance to tobacco vein mottling and tobacco etch viruses. Because those diseases were so widespread in the region, the average yield at the Tobacco Experiment Station improved over three hundred pounds per acre simply by switching to the use of TN 86. Now, most modern burley tobacco varieties have virus resistance derived from TN 86.

I have spent much of my career trying to improve resistance to race 1 black shank. Even before I began working in Tennessee, this area has been notorious for black shank. It is much worse here than in Kentucky. Why? Many farmers here irrigate, and that can spread the disease. In fact, anything that moves soil and water can move black shank. Farm equipment moving from one field to another frequently is the reason for its spread, and over time, the disease will build up in the soil. Add the fact that farmers here frequently used no rotation due to the lack of available land suitable for tobacco production, and black shank soon became an epidemic.

In some tobacco-production areas, the race 0 strain of black shank could be controlled by varieties that contained a single gene that came from *Nicotiana longiflora*. But development of single gene resistance for black shank came with a price: it led to the development of the race 1 strain of black shank that could overcome that resistance, and race 1 eventually became the dominant strain, particularly in Tennessee. However, we have made tremendous progress in developing new varieties that have good resistance to race 1 black shank. By using the newer varieties and including even minimal crop rotation, black shank can now be essentially controlled during most growing seasons.

In 1999, the Universities of Kentucky and Tennessee merged their tobacco-breeding programs to form the Kentucky-Tennessee Tobacco Improvement Initiative (KTTII), which has been very successful. By combining land resources and personnel between the two states, the breeding program has become much more efficient. The tobacco industry loves the multistate breeding program. It can put all its resources in one program. It has worked tremendously well. It was the first university program that was entirely collaborative between two states. Currently, KTTII is the leading burley breeding program in the world.

Breeding will continue to be important to burley production in the future. Kentucky, Tennessee, southwestern Virginia and western North Carolina are still among the best regions in the world for the production of burley tobacco. However, if we did not have the disease resistance in burley tobacco varieties that has been achieved through university research, we couldn't successfully grow tobacco in these areas. Unfortunately, new tobacco diseases such as target spot and tomato spotted wilt virus seem to constantly be arriving on the scene, necessitating the need for continued research. The sad reality in plant breeding is that you never seem to catch up to the point that everything is under control.

JEFF AIKEN, FARMER, TEDFORD, TENNESSEE

You know, one of the things that really sticks in my memory about growing up on a tobacco farm is how on Thanksgiving Day, everyone in my family would gather in the barn and strip tobacco.

Left: "Tobacco growing may have been more romantic in days gone by, but tobacco is a business now," says Jeff Aiken, a farmer in Tedford, Tennessee. *Photo by Chris Bickers.*

Below: Some years Aiken cures burley in this old multitier barn. *Photo by Chris Bickers.*

Greenhouse plant production has been one of the great advances in tobacco technology in the last fifty years. Aiken stands in one of his houses. *Photo by Chris Bickers.*

While we were stripping, stories abounded, and often someone would have the radio on. I remember many Saturday afternoons when we would listen to the UT football games. Working in tobacco, especially when stripping, is somewhat confined. Everyone was in one area. Fellowship was forced on you, you might say.

The family atmosphere is no longer the same on a burley farm. Now we grow such a large number of acres that we have to hire outside help. It is not the same.

There were valuable lessons learned for a young person growing up in the tobacco field, although I have to admit that at the time, they didn't seem that important. At the time, I didn't realize the value of it.

When I was a kid, we would pass each stalk down from one person to the next. Everyone would pull one grade. This was quite a job since we would often pull seven or eight grades. When I first started working in tobacco, when I was five or six, the only thing they would let me do was to strip the last grade. I felt I had really done something when they let me pull another grade.

We grade several different ways now. We can each strip a full stalk, or we can hand it down, or I have a chain system where you can pull with both hands. Sometimes we strip into five or six grades, sometimes two or three, dependent on the crop and what the buyer wants. The first year I used migrants, I paid my workers by the pound to strip. But I don't seem to get as good grade separation as when I pay by the hour.

I am at least the third generation of my family that has been associated with burley in Tennessee. My grandpa had tobacco as far back as I know of.

After he died, tobacco was all my grandmother had to provide for her and her family. My dad bought the farm from my grandmother. Once I got out of school, I wanted to be a farmer myself. For any young man around here, that generally meant tobacco.

Forty years ago, I guess in a lot of ways they took more pride in what they were producing than folks do now. Efficiency and yield are more important than quality. Tobacco is still profitable. But the margin is significantly lower now. I don't know that the product was that much higher in quality then. I would have to think about that. But I do know that it took more time to produce back then. There was more tender loving care.

One lesson I learned early on was that if you leave your burley out after you cut it for three nights and three dews, that will take the sunburn out.

The biggest change in burley production since I first began has been how we produce plants. I can remember that the first pretty day in February, Dad would always want to get started on his plant beds. I can remember pulling weeds out of the bed on my hands and knees. When they were ready to go to the field, we would have to stop pulling plants at two or three o'clock, then take them to the field and set them. Now we can set all day if we want to. And there's a different attitude now to the weather. Now if it rains, we can wait till it dries up. Back then, we wanted to plant when it was wet because it was easier.

Another big difference is the change we have made in going to bales. When I was a teenager, we left baskets and went to one-hundred-pound bales. Since then, we have adopted seven-hundred-pound bales.

There was a time when Greene was the largest burley-producing county in the state. It was not because it had huge producers—it didn't. It was the volume of producers. There were many, most on a small scale. I grow about one hundred acres of burley now. When I was a kid, five or six acres was considered a lot.

I have heard it said that all the romance has gone out of tobacco and now it is just economics. But you have to look at tobacco as a business or you won't be in it long.

3

HOW THE QUOTA BUYOUT IMPACTED BURLEY FARMERS

BY WILLIAM THOMAS JARRETT

In the fall of 2006, I began conducting interviews with tobacco farmers in Tennessee, North Carolina and Virginia to see how they had been impacted differently by the buyout. These interviews were done in three different areas: Sullivan County, Tennessee (county seat, Blountville); Washington County, Virginia (county seat, Abingdon); and Watauga County, North Carolina (county seat, Boone). Historically, all had depended heavily on the burley tobacco industry for a majority of their income. I determined both the positive and negative impacts that the buyout brought to these different locations. Following is a summation of what I learned, with short interviews from farmers that illustrate my findings.

The average age of tobacco farmers in this tri-state study was sixty years, ranging from thirty-five to eighty-four years with statistics showing the average age of Tennessee farmers as fifty-seven. The years of involvement in agriculture averaged forty-eight and a half or more years per farmer. Out of a total of thirty-two tobacco farmers, only ten strictly farmed with no other income.

Out of the thirty-two participants in this study, thirteen produced a tobacco crop in 2005—the first year after the quota cuts and price support were terminated. These farmers averaged $1.62 per pound for their crop when it was sold in 2005. North Carolina had the highest-marketed average at $1.69, and Tennessee had the lowest at $1.57, with Virginia in the middle at $1.60. Participation in the buyout program was 100 percent with the exception of one farmer in North Carolina.

In all three states, the general consensus was: the buyout would be most beneficial to older farmers nearing retirement who were too old to continue producing tobacco anyway and to those with significant acreage history. The older farmers were the most willing to give up the practice. One common aspect associated with the data gathered from these interviews was the benefit that migrant labor had brought to the tobacco industry. All participants talked of how this labor had been a positive force that kept tobacco production going in the past decade.

One of the farmers in Sullivan County, Tennessee, commented on how the balance of cattle and burley on many farms would probably be impacted:

> *In the beef cattle business and tobacco, when the cattle price was down, you could fall back on tobacco, and break even for the year, or come out. Then when tobacco didn't do good, you had your cattle. But now, cattle prices are high, but when they go down, which they eventually will, and you don't have your tobacco there to fall back on, I think that will put a whole lot of small farmers plumb out of farming, not just tobacco farming, but plumb out of the cattle business or small farms. Just won't have the money to survive without tobacco's filling in the bad years of other crops and things.*

The buyout would be of very little benefit to smaller farmers without much acreage, he said. "The larger farmers would benefit, but what hurt most was that all farmers should have been paid when they were at maximum production during the late '90s."

"I don't think the buyout will have any effect on the economy as far as boosting it," said my second Tennessee gamer.

> *The biggest effect on the economy in this area would be the loss of the tobacco altogether. A lot of equipment places that sold farm equipment, most of the farm equipment was [bought] with tobacco money. Automobiles, a lot was bought with tobacco money. Taxes, land property taxes, was paid with what people made on their tobacco. And the loss of tobacco will make a big impact in this area. As far as the farmer, the foreign market is just really what put your tobacco out. Probably in the '60s, or around 1970, the U.S. raised 86 percent of the tobacco in the world. And before we started getting quota cuts, we was raising 26 percent in the world, which was probably in the 1990s. We was raising the same amount of tobacco, but only 26 percent of the world's supply. So you can tell how much Brazil and all these other countries have really raised a lot more tobacco. In the last*

twenty years, they don't have any control, like they do on the farmers' here, and their expenses is not near as big, their labor is cheap, they don't have to use a lot of the chemicals. Can raise it a lot cheaper than we can.

Another Sullivan County farmer said:

I think there's a lot of people that have gone out of the tobacco business because of the buyout. A lot of them would have gone out anyway, whether they would have had the buyout or not. I think that some of the farm families that are not growing tobacco are gonna miss that income that comes in from their tobacco crop. The companies are still wanting tobacco, domestic and international companies are still looking for the quality of tobacco that we produce in the United States. I think tobacco will continue to be grown in the U.S., maybe not as much of it in the historical areas as was in the past; I think that the reduction in price will allow it to be more competitive in the international market. But I think the price is gonna have to come up from what it has been from the last year or two in order to get the tobacco grown because I think some of the new growers in the nontraditional burley areas are finding out how much work there is in harvesting and producing the burley crop. So they're probably not gonna be as enthusiastic about it as they were the first year before they tried it, before they tried growing the crop. I still think, in the long run, the buyout was probably a good thing for this part of the U.S., the burley belt area, because it gave people who had historically grown tobacco the chance to get some income.

And another Tennessee burley grower said, "I think it's definitely going to hurt the economy of the small farmers for years to come, even though you're getting a little buyout money. It does help, but I think that over the long haul, the small burley [producer] will lose money. It was definitely a loss to the community, yes."

The North Carolina farmers, all from the Boone area, had similar opinions about the buyout.

"[It's] the worst thing that's ever came out of Washington since the welfare program," said one.

Farmers that did raise tobacco that just had an acre or so, they just plumb quit. And I would probably quit, too, but I've got obligations that carry on that I have to raise the tobacco. The tobacco buyout, they've got it set up for ten years. I'm forty-seven, and I still got years to work. Tobacco buyout *should have been upfront, one shot. Use that money to invest. I get less than $1,000 a year from the tobacco buyout. And it probably cost me $1,800 to $2,000 when the government dropped out of it on account of the price support. You had too many people controlling what was going on in the tobacco business that had no incentive to grow tobacco. But they controlled the tobacco cards, and they were making decisions based on their own personal ideals instead of trying to make it work out for all the farmers.*

Another North Carolinian said:

Being a farmer that produces it and buying quota, I think we should have gotten a bigger piece of the pie. Because most of your quota holders don't know what tobacco is. They just bought a piece of property that had a quota on it. In my opinion, the farmer [grower] *should have got a bigger piece* [than the quota holder]. *In a lot of cases, the grower should have had more because had it not been for the grower leasing poundage and growing it, a lot of quota holders would have not grown it anyway for years and years. So the grower should have had more.*

One of the Virginia farmers said he thinks that the buyout price was roughly half of what the value of quota had been at its peak. "It is just about half, or less than half, of what it was when they started talking about [the buyout]," he said. "You kept cutting everyone's allotment down to I guess where they wanted it. I don't know that for a fact, but everybody got half what they [would have gotten] seven or eight years ago."

Another Virginian said that tobacco had been a great boon in the Abingdon area. "It's paid for a lot of farms, bought a lot of houses, sent a lot of kids to school, college…most anything that you have, as farm people, is attributed to tobacco."

And a third Virginia farmer said, "I think it's greatly benefited our economy. I know people around here that's got factory jobs, and before the buyout came along, [they] raised a little bit of tobacco to help pay for their taxes at the end of the year. I think it's going to be hard for this area to find something that can do that for them."

Besides the farmers, I interviewed two agriculture agents in Virginia. Both agents talked with fondness about how the tobacco industry benefited the state of Virginia. One summarized it this way: "Tobacco has been the main source of income here in Washington County for years. A family could take a tobacco base [and] live on that income; they could educate their children.

A good tobacco base would provide an income for a family to live on and live with reasonable wealth. There is no other crop or no other industry here that's done that."

And speaking of the children, of the thirty-two families involved in the survey, only two included children who were interested in farming as their life's profession. Only one of those was old enough at the time to actually consider this option as a career and put it into action.

Some final points I learned from these interviews:

Many of the farmers in this study expressed concern that if it were not for the Mexicans (for not only farm labor but also general manual labor), the whole nation would be in trouble. Time and time again, the farmers in all three states addressed the situation of not being able to get anyone to work—not only were helpers not willing, but they were also unable, not just physically unable but also unskilled for the type of labor required by those who farm. Meaning, if you are not raised up with it, most likely you cannot do it.

Those who perceived the buyout positively generally had owned their quotas and raised them themselves, thus allowing them to receive the seven-dollar quota holder share plus the three-dollar producer/grower share. Again, by being in this position and also by continuing to raise significant acreage up until the years of the buyout, they stood to receive substantial funds simply because they were not just the grower or just the quota holder but both.

I feel the future of the domestic tobacco market for the three states in this study is at best bleak. The farmers who were brave enough to raise a crop in 2005 after the 2004 buyout with no price support were, for the most part, dissatisfied with the price they received. Any who plan on continuing to produce tobacco over the next few years stated that they would cut production significantly unless the price increased, and that is not likely.

Note: This report is based on a thesis written for a sociology degree at East Tennessee State University. I would like to acknowledge several people who have assisted: Dr. Martha Copp, Dr. Lindsey King and, particularly, Dr. Scott Beck, all from ETSU, for their help and support, and the many tobacco farmers and their families for their cooperation in agreeing to be interviewed for this study. But first and foremost, I wish to thank my parents, Ronald D. and Teresa Thomas Jarrett, and our extended family for their help and encouragement over the many years. The completion of these degrees has been somewhat of a challenge because I struggle with two disabilities. I have been legally blind since birth and a juvenile diabetic since the age of eight.

4

HOW GROWERS CREATED A STABLE MARKET

THE CREATION OF THE BURLEY STABILIZATION CORPORATION

The cigarette industry as we know it today emerged in 1913. The most popular brands sold for fifteen cents per pack. A new blend was introduced with flue-cured, burley and some Turkish and sold for ten cents per pack. By 1930, Reynolds, American and Liggett and Myers controlled over 90 percent of the market. Lorillard was late in developing a standard brand and never captured more than 7 percent of the market.

Prices for tobacco in the 1890s ranged between eight and twelve cents per pound for grades medium or better. By 1904, prices had dropped to three cents and lower. Growers' discontent led to the formation of organizations designed to increase grower bargaining power with a price goal of eight cents a pound. In 1904, growers in the Dark District of Kentucky and Tennessee formed the Dark-District Planters Protective Association. Buyers, in an attempt to break up the association, offered growers twelve cents per pound if they would not honor their contracts. In 1906, the Night Riders were formed to keep the growers in line. From 1906 to 1909, this campaign to influence prices through threats extended throughout the burley area.

As a result, the Burley Tobacco Society was formed in 1907, and the Interstate Tobacco Growers Protective Association was organized in Virginia and North Carolina. As its main objective, if price demands were not met, the association planned to re-dry, store and hold the tobacco until

The Burley Stabilization Corporation's Daniel Green at the cooperative's office in Springfield, Tennessee. *Photo by Chris Bickers.*

the price was met. With the coming of World War I, the demand for tobacco increased. Prices peaked in 1919, averaging thirty-one cents per pound for all tobacco. This strong market situation resulted in a subsiding of interest in the cooperative effort, and growers left the associations.

However, by 1920, prices had dropped in Kentucky from twenty-four cents to eleven cents and in North Carolina from forty-nine cents to twenty-one cents. Interest in the cooperative movement was renewed. In 1921, the Burley Tobacco Growers Cooperative Association was formed. This was followed in 1922 by the Tobacco Growers Association of North and South Carolina and Virginia (Tri-State).

The objective of the Tri-State Association was to obtain monopoly power and thus set the prices for its leaf. Under an ironclad contract, the growers would hand over their tobacco to the cooperative, which would grade, re-dry and store it. The crop would be held off the market until a favorable time for selling. The growers received an advance payment when they delivered their crop and a second payment when the tobacco was sold. Merchants, bankers and businessmen generally professed sympathy for the movement. Extension workers and students in the state agricultural colleges worked enthusiastically at securing pledges. However, at least 43 percent of annual production remained under the control of farmers who refused to join the movement. Clarence Poe, editor of *Progressive Farmer*, wrote that "speculators and parasites who fatten on the present system [auction sales]" were trying to mislead farmers with "insinuations, falsehoods and twisted half truths."

Basically, the manufacturers supported the co-op. James B. Duke wished to see cooperative marketing win out in tobacco so the farmers would not plant more than the world could consume. However, the warehouse interest, strongly backed by leaf dealers and the time merchants, pressed the growers to desert the cooperative and offered the benefit of paying the grower the full price immediately rather than the partial initial payment offered by the cooperative. By 1926, the Tri-State had failed.

Financing production was an ongoing problem. Most farmers needed yearlong credit and were in debt from January through December. Banks were reluctant to make short-term credit available to farmers, who instead had to turn to one of the standard institutions of the tobacco belt: the time merchant.

The time merchants provided farmers with general supplies and fertilizer on credit, charging not only high rates of interest but also credit prices, which were considerably higher than prices for cash payment. The cost of short-term credit, which banks would not provide, was extremely high. In 1926, the time merchants were charging an interest rate of 25 percent per year. Fertilizer manufacturers charged an even higher rate. About 75 percent of the tenants' cash gain had to be used to pay back cash advances from landlords and settle accounts with the time merchant.

Tobacco farmers were also handicapped by a weak marketing position. Their basic inability to adjust supply to demand created a chronic tendency to overproduce. Good prices always led to increased production the following year. When prices fell, however, there was not necessarily an equivalent cutback in production. Farmers responded to lower prices by slightly curtailing acreage or even increasing production in an effort to minimize total losses. The prices buyers paid for tobacco depended on how they graded it. These grades were secret, and they varied from company to company so that the farmer had no way of knowing whether he was receiving a fair price for his tobacco. In addition, the manufacturers maintained a three-year inventory. If in any year the crop was short, pushing prices up, they did not have to buy at the higher prices. They could afford to wait. The grower could not. Richard Russell, governor of Georgia, stated that the price paid for tobacco in his state in 1932 forced him to conclude that the manufacturers of tobacco had as complete a monopoly as this nation had ever seen.

Prices, which never fell below 20.0 cents per pound from 1920 to 1927, dropped to 17.3 cents in 1928, 12.0 cents in 1930 and 8.4 cents in 1931.

Growers responded to these low prices by voting for production controls and direct payments in 1933, forming the basis of the Federal Tobacco Program, which remained in effect until 2004.

But there were a few bumps in the road. Several acts were passed in Congress in 1933 and 1934 to provide production controls and price protection. In 1936, the Supreme Court ruled these acts unconstitutional. This led to the passage of the Agricultural Adjustment Act of 1938. This act, which became the basis of the program, provided for a marketing quota and authorized payments for the difference between parity price (based on the 1919–29 period) and market price. Marketing quotas in any given year required approval by two-thirds of the growers. Quotas were approved for 1938. The loan level was 75 percent of parity for flue-cured tobacco.

Growers rejected quotas in 1939 and produced the largest crop ever. Prices fell, and production controls were voted back in the next year. Legislation was also passed to provide for a minimum price to be placed on each government standard grade. Farm leadership and USDA officials determined that growers should be responsible for the implementation and operation of the program through the establishment of grower cooperatives.

The co-op concept was to provide a mechanism through which loans can be made to its members and through which tobacco that served as collateral for the loan was received, processed, stored and sold. The basic philosophy was that growers would operate and administer their program, and further, through this plan, their program could be operated on a self-sustaining basis at no cost to the USDA. The overall effect of the program is that it provides the grower with a stabilized and orderly marketing system that eliminates drastic fluctuations in market price.

Price supports established minimum prices farmers could receive for their tobacco. The average price support level was influenced by changes in the previous year's market prices and farmers' costs of production. Farmers delivered their tobacco to auction warehouses where government graders (financed by the farmers) placed a grade on each sales lot of tobacco. If tobacco companies did not bid one cent per pound above the government-established price support level, the tobacco was purchased by the cooperative. Price supports provided farmers with a stable market without drastic fluctuations in market price at a time when they were needed.

The cooperative paid the farmer using money borrowed from the USDA. The tobacco represented collateral on the government-backed loan. The cooperatives had the tobacco processed and stored for future sale. Following the sale of the tobacco, the cooperative repaid the loans in full plus accrued interest.

Burley Stabilization Corporation was incorporated on July 16, 1953. It was formed for the purpose of handling the price support program for burley tobacco and providing support to Tennessee burley growers. In 1958, at the request of the USDA-CCC, the area of operation was extended to cover the burley markets in western North Carolina. In 1971, the area of operations was extended to cover burley markets in southwest Virginia.

By the late 1940s, burley production in the United States was increasing rapidly, making it difficult for burley producers in Tennessee to find an efficient means to handle excess production. The Federal Tobacco Program provided a system whereby cooperatives could purchase excess production and store the tobacco until the market provided an outlet. By the early 1950s, the Flue-Cured Tobacco Cooperative in North Carolina and the Burley Tobacco Growers Cooperative in Kentucky had been serving tobacco farmers in their respective regions for approximately ten years, but because of the geographic distance and difficulty of transport, there existed a great need for growers in Tennessee to organize their own cooperative.

BSC continued to play an important role in the administration of the Federal Tobacco Program for more than fifty years. The Federal Tobacco Program was quite successful for most of its existence, providing for stable prices by adjusting supplies each year. BSC would borrow money from the USDA, then process, store and sell the tobacco and repay the loans.

The Federal Tobacco Program was very successful when the United States dominated the world tobacco production share, but it also resulted in higher prices each year, which allowed foreign producers to gain production share each year until the program was no longer effective. The solution was to eliminate the non-value added cost of leasing and get the production rights into the hands of the growers by doing away with the Federal Tobacco Program.

The Fair and Equitable Tobacco Reform Act of 2004 (P.L. 108-357), signed by President Bush on October 22, 2004, ended the Federal Tobacco Program. That meant the role of BSC had to change, and it did.

The most significant step was probably the decision to move BSC headquarters from its home of fifty years in Knoxville. The new location was Springfield, Tennessee, about thirty miles north of Nashville. It was a two-hundred-mile move, but the decision proved a wise one to get closer to its primary production area.

"The geographic distribution of burley production in the three states we traditionally served changed after the buyout," Daniel Green, BSC

A worker loads processed burley in boxes at the warehouse of the Burley Stabilization Corporation's main office in Springfield, Tennessee. *Photo by Chris Bickers.*

After the buyout, burley production began in states far from the traditional production zones, as on the Lancaster County, Pennsylvania farm shown here. *Photo by Chris Bickers.*

chief executive officer, explained at the time. "It seemed wise to put our operational headquarters in middle Tennessee, where it would be in closer proximity to the chief burley producing area."

The Burley Stabilization Corporation had been located in Knoxville from its founding. It was a satisfactory location for most of that time. But after deregulation, it was soon clear that plantings were going to shift, probably north and west of Knoxville.

Springfield, where the cooperative already owned some storage facilities, seemed a better hub for its activities. But BSC didn't abandon its mountain and Tennessee Valley farmers. The cooperative obtained a warehouse in Greeneville in eastern Tennessee to continue to serve its members there and in neighboring North Carolina and Virginia.

Since the buyout, BSC has also significantly increased its operations in Kentucky and has contracted with farmers from as far east as Pennsylvania and as far west as Missouri.

How Research Has Strengthened Burley Production

By Charles Click

In the spring of 1928, Clyde B. Austin, founder of the Austin Tobacco Company, asked the University of Tennessee to consider establishing a tobacco research facility in Greeneville, Tennessee. Along with a number of other prominent tobacco men, Austin believed that the state needed a tobacco research station and that the location should be in the state's leading burley tobacco–growing county. The idea took practical shape during the 1930–31 session of the state legislature. A bill was passed granting $25,000 for the purchase of land on which a tobacco research station would be established. This facility would be a cooperative effort between the University of Tennessee and the United States Department of Agriculture's office of Tobacco and Plant Nutrition. In a called session of the legislature, this appropriation, along with others, was reduced by 15 percent, a reflection of the economically depressed times.

The University of Tennessee Research and Education Center in Greeneville, Tennessee, has helped farmers adopt improved practices since 1932. *Photo courtesy of the UT Institute of Agriculture.*

The actual site of the Tobacco Experiment Station was selected in the fall of 1931 by a committee representing the U.S. Department of Agriculture, the University of Tennessee and prominent Greeneville tobacco warehousemen. Members of this committee included W.M. Garner, of the U.S. Department of Agriculture; C.A. Mooers, director of the University of Tennessee Experiment Station; and Clyde B. Austin, W.F. Russell, D.T. Jones and A.J. Stephens, local tobacco men. This same group of local tobacco men signed a note for $1,542.68 in July 1932 to help the station pay off a debt owed to the First National Bank of Greeneville. This gesture, along with subsequent aid given by these men, showed the faith and interest they had in the establishment of the station. The site chosen for the station was located about five miles south of Greeneville and consisted of 163 acres. Of this acreage, 149 were purchased from F.C. Wilhoit and 14 from Frank Williams. The Wilhoit property had two houses, two barns and a granary. The property, watered by Richland Creek and a very large spring, was composed of gently rolling land and fertile creek bottomland.

The Tobacco Experiment Station opened in the spring of 1932. F.C. Wilhoit was hired as farm foreman with a crew of twenty men. This crew was soon busy cleaning up the farm and preparing ground for that season's crops. Old fence rows were torn out and replaced; ground was cleared and grubbed by hand while heavier work was performed by horses and mules. The work was hard, with the average week at fifty-five hours per man. For this week's work, the men received about $7.50. This was a decent wage in Greene County in the 1930s, and most of the men were glad to have a steady job. Besides the Tobacco Experiment Station, Pet Milk Company and Austin Tobacco Company were the only other places in Greene County where public jobs could be found.

In February 1932, Frank S. Chance was appointed superintendent of the Tobacco Experiment Station. Prior to accepting this position, Chance had been a banker in Knoxville, had taught at the University of Tennessee and had been a county agriculture agent. His background in agriculture and his work at the Tobacco Experiment Station led to him being referred to as the "champion burley tobacco grower of the nation." Chance served as the station's superintendent for eleven years, during which time the station grew from one man's idea into one of the leading agricultural research facilities in the Southeast.

When the Wilhoit farm was acquired by the University of Tennessee, the land was in poor condition. Like much of the farmland in the Tennessee River Valley, the ground was poor because previous farmers had failed to follow the practice of crop rotation and had not been able to fertilize because of the margin of crop costs set against low agricultural prices. The failure or inability to follow proper farming practices resulted in another problem that plagued the Tennessee Valley at this time. Years of soil erosion had left huge gullies in many of the fields. In order to begin fighting the soil erosion problem, Chance obtained twenty-four pounds of sericia seed, valued at ten dollars per pound, from the Knoxville station. Sericia was highly prized as a deterrent to soil erosion, and Chance valued the seed so much that he placed it in the station's safe until time for its planting.

Equipment needs for the station became one of Chance's early priorities. Bids for equipment were accepted from various local firms, including Russell, Campbell and Tucker Hardware of Greeneville and Treadway Seed and Feed Company of Johnson City. Some of the items purchased at this time were a manure spreader for $131.00, a cultipacker for $62.50 and a Van Brunt grain drill for $250.00. All of the initial equipment purchased for the station was of the horse- and mule-drawn variety since the station could not afford a tractor at this time. There is a reference in Chance's diary concerning the hiring of Frank Williams to turn ground with his tractor for a fee of $2.50 per acre, but most of the farm's work was performed through horse and mule power. The housing and feeding of the farm's draft animals was a prime concern during this period. Although all the farm's crew was familiar with how to work and care for these animals, certain individuals in the crew proved to be better with these animals than did others. Thus, there evolved to a certain extent a group of specialists who did most of the work with the horses and mules. These draft animals, along with the other livestock on the farm, provided the station with another service besides labor. The use of manure for fertilization was as necessary for the station as it was for the average farmer. A test comparing manure with commercial fertilizer was one of the first experiments conducted at the station.

Work to get the 1932 crop of tobacco out began with the preparation of plant beds. Once the site for the plant bed was plowed and worked down, the men piled huge quantities of dry brush on the beds and set it ablaze. This was done in an effort to sterilize the soil against weeds and disease. After the brush was burned off, the beds were raked to a smooth finish, and the tobacco seeds, mixed with stove ashes or lime, were strewn by hand over the bed. Many growers would then firm the seeds into the soil by tromping the beds with their feet or using a heavy roller. A light covering of straw was used to help hold moisture, and a light cotton cover was placed over the beds to protect the seedlings from the elements. The beds were carefully watched for signs of insect damage, disease, weeds and lack of moisture. If all went well, the tobacco plants would be ready to transplant into the field in about sixty days. According to Superintendent Chance's records, May 20, 1932, was the date on which the first tobacco was planted at the station. Chance reported that 1,500 plants were pegged out in the South Field. Although he does not specify how long it took to transplant this number of plants, one can assume that it took the better part of a day because of the method used in setting. Pegging tobacco is a slow, backbreaking process in which a stick is used to make a hole in the ground—preferably when it is muddy. The plant is placed in this hole, and the stick is used to firm the soil around the roots.

Once the tobacco was transplanted into the fields and began growing, the station's experimental work began in earnest. The most vital research conducted at the station in these early years dealt with a plant disease known as black root rot. This disease, which is a soil-borne fungus, cost burley tobacco growers millions of dollars annually. As its name implies, black root rot attacks the root system of a tobacco plant, robbing the plant of its ability to sustain itself. Although the disease does not always kill the affected plant, the resulting stunting cuts yields drastically. Since the disease remains in the soil and is increased in strength every time tobacco is grown in that soil, the most natural countermeasure was crop rotation. This method was not always practical in the hilly terrain of east Tennessee, where good tobacco ground was often scarce. Therefore, planters needed another solution. Previous studies found that certain varieties of tobacco showed varying degrees of resistance to black root rot. While these varieties showed resistance, most were only a generation or two removed from their wild state, leaving much to be desired in both their quality and size. Research at the station began to focus on developing varieties that were not only resistant to black root rot but also would produce leaves of the size and quality desired by burley growers everywhere.

Chance's records show that fifteen tobacco varieties were screened in this early black root rot test. Varieties known to be susceptible to the disease were planted on one side of a field that was known to be infested with black root rot while resistant varieties were planted on the opposite side of the field. The varieties were flip-flopped the following year with the more resistant varieties being planted in the soil where the disease had been increased by the susceptible varieties. Individual plants showing a high level of resistance to the disease were selected and crossed with varieties that met the requirements for size and quality. Seeds from these plants were saved for the following year's crop, and the selection and crossing process continued. Insight into the nature of this work can be gained by the fact that it was not until 1950, when Burley 1 was released, that a variety of tobacco resistant to black root rot was found.

Although the research conducted at the Tobacco Experiment Station was of a purely scientific nature, the actual work and cultivation practices performed by the station were the same as those performed by tobacco farmers. Tobacco, as well as row crops such as corn, were grown on ridges made by bringing dirt up against the plant with a hoe. Keeping the tobacco patches free from weeds required many man-hours of using a hoe and following a mule pulling a "three-foot" plow. Insect and sucker control were also quite different from today's wide use of chemicals. Bud worms, which are very destructive to tobacco, were manually picked off each plant and squashed or dusted with a combination of arsenate of lead and corn meal. Sucker control was also done by hand with each plant having to be suckered three or four times before harvest.

Harvesting of the first tobacco crop grown at the station began on August 19, 1932. This aspect of tobacco farming has changed little throughout the years. The work is dirty and requires a great deal of physical effort. The plants are cut off close to the ground and placed on sticks, which are hung in a curing barn. Tobacco cutting time brought communities together with neighbors helping one another with the harvest. Farmers took pride in how well they performed the various tasks required in harvesting the crop. Some individuals specialized in jobs such as packing a wagon or spearing the plants onto a stick. The tobacco harvest was an integral part of east Tennesseans' culture.

On November 1, 1932, preparing the tobacco for market began at the station. In those days, the leaves were placed into six different grades based on color and quality. The number of grades was greater then than in today's market because the filterless cigarettes required more blending of tobaccos in order to reduce harshness. The six grades were given names to describe their characteristics. "Tips" were short dark leaves at the very top of the stalk. "Short red," the set of leaves below the tips, were dark red and short bodied. "Long red," next on the stalk, were, as the name implies, the long, dark red leaves. "Bright leaf" was the grade most sought by buyers in those days because its bright color and smooth texture made it an excellent cigarette blend. The "lugs" were below the bright leaf on the stalk; this grade was light in color and in body and was next to bright leaf in desirability. The "flyings" or "trash lugs," the very bottom leaves on the stalk, were light in both color and body and were of marginal use to the tobacco companies.

The first tobacco to be sold from the experiment station was on December 19, 1932, at the Planters Warehouse Number Two in Greeneville, Tennessee.

Sold on that date were 226 pounds of tips at 5.5 cents per pound, 256 pounds of short red at 15.0 cents per pound, 292 pounds of long red at 18.5 cents per pound, 332 pounds of bright leaf at 23.5 cents per pound, 272 pounds of lugs at 23.5 cents per pound and 320 pounds of flyings at 18.0 cents per pound. Compared to the current market, these prices seem ridiculous. However, at a time when cash money was hard to come by, farm families felt fortunate to have a tobacco market. In 1932, the Tobacco Experiment Station sold a total of 4,040 pounds of tobacco for the price of $587.25, an average of 14.5 cents per pound.

Work at the station progressed quite well through the early years. By the end of 1933, the farm's crew had constructed four houses and two barns. The houses were for members of the farm's crew and their families, while one of the barns was for livestock and the other for housing tobacco. The need for a new tobacco barn had been precipitated by a fire in the summer of 1932 that destroyed one of the station's barns. This fire was caused through the spontaneous combustion of hay that had been put in the barn too green. The blaze destroyed several tons of hay and a large quantity of tobacco housed in the barn. The estimated loss caused by this fire was $2,500.

Much of the lumber used in the construction of these two new barns was sawed from timber cut on the farm's property. The use of trees for timber and fence posts was essential during these early years. In fact, locust fence posts were judged to be so vital that several hundred locust trees were planted just for this purpose. The station's growth was aided through the sale of timber and various other crops grown on the farm. This was needed because of the extremely depressed prices of the tobacco crop. The farm's 1933 tobacco crop totaled 10,256 pounds and sold for $1,123.48 for an average of a little over nine cents per pound. Poor quality was cited as the reason for the low price, with many piles of tobacco being passed over by the buyers, brought back home and used as fertilizer or as lining in potato cellars. While the prices paid for the farm's crops were low, the money received did have a good deal of purchasing power. Evidence of this is found in the purchase of a new 1934 Ford sedan for $714.06. The car was to be used by Chance in the discharge of his duties as superintendent of the Tobacco Experiment Station.

The times were hard economically, but they were not so bad in other ways. There was a closeness of family and community that was reflected in all areas of life. This closeness was seen in the various social gatherings within the community. Large crowds gathered for events such as ice cream suppers, cakewalks, county league baseball games and church revival meetings, all of which provided entertainment.

THE ROLE OF THE FIELD DAY

The experiment station played a role in the community's social scene through its annual Field Days. This event, which began on August 12, 1932, was a showcase for the work being conducted at the station. Farmers were given a tour, and programs dealing with the station's work were presented. Field days during the early years were more than just a means of passing out information. They were social events that brought huge crowds to the station to enjoy a picnic lunch, a band concert and a variety of other forms of entertainment.

On August 11, 1933, the station held its second Field Day. The highlight of this Field Day was a tour of the newly constructed tobacco barn. This barn, hailed as the "model burley tobacco barn," was toured by farmers from twelve east Tennessee counties. The new barn was ninety-six feet long, thirty-six feet wide and seven tiers high in the center. The barn was tiered lengthwise with three driveways running the length of the barn, which allowed for more speed in the housing process. The "new burley barn" was capable of holding up to six thousand sticks of tobacco and had hinged doors along the walls every four and a half feet for ventilation. This barn, which is still called the new burley barn, continues to serve the purpose for which it was originally constructed.

As with other Field Days during the early years of the station, lunch was provided, and there was also a variety of entertainment. A singing group known as the Burley Quartet seemed to have been the crowd pleaser that

The Field Day is an important method of disseminating information acquired at the center, still affectionately known as the "Tobacco Experiment Station." *Photo courtesy of the UT Institute of Agriculture.*

Burley is "hung" in a conventional barn on the grounds of the Greeneville Research and Education Center in 1999. *Photo by Chris Bickers.*

year. According to a newspaper account of the event, the group, composed of Wayland Wilhoit, Dean Wilhoit, Glenn Wilhoit and Herman Burgner, entertained the large crowd with a variety of songs ranging from the current hits of the day to the old standards. Reports indicate that the farmers were impressed with the work going on at the station, and most felt that it was a worthwhile venture. "The success of this 1933 Field Day is somewhat amazing," according to a letter from Superintendent Chance to Mr. J.C. McAmis of the Agricultural Extension Service. Chance reflects on the difficulties he faced in establishing the station and reveals to McAmis that not one of the scheduled speakers for the event arrived that day. Instead, Chance, along with McAmis and Dean C.A. Wellson of the University of Tennessee, had carried out the program. Difficulties such as these coupled with the economic uncertainties of the 1930s often tested Chance's resolve in the initial years of the station's growth.

In October 1933, Chance filed a request with the Reconstruction Finance Corporation asking for assistance in the construction of roads on the experiment station. This request was the beginning of an association between the experiment station and a variety of New Deal agencies that would last until the end of the 1930s. In addition to assistance from the RFC, the station received aid from the Works Progress Administration, the Tennessee Emergency Relief Association, the Civil Works Administration, the Civilian Conservation Corps and the Tennessee Valley Authority. Workers from these agencies worked on a variety of projects on the station, including the building of roads and erosion dams, the construction of barns and houses and the blasting of rocks and stumps out of the farm's fields. The agencies also provided funds and equipment for various station projects. While it cannot be stated for certain that the New Deal agencies saved the experiment station, it is almost a certainty that its growth would have been greatly retarded without their aid. This statement holds true for all of Greene County as well, for even though people often scoffed at the men who worked for these agencies, their impact (in most instances) was positive. Evidence of this can still be seen in Greene County, where a number of New Deal projects, including a large school, continue to be used. In addition, the economic impact of payrolls—the WPA employed over six hundred men in Greene County—and equipment purchases had to have a positive effect on the county.

In December 1933, Chance applied to the Civil Works Administration for labor to be used in various projects on the farm. The CWA approved the request and sent a crew of six men to the farm. These men performed a variety of tasks, including cutting timber, building barns and constructing concrete bridges. One of the barns built by the CWA workmen was used to house the farm's mules and horses. Known as the "mule barn," it had concrete flooring and individual stalls for the animals. There was also a large hayloft and a granary in the barn. Although no longer used to house livestock, the barn today is in sound condition and continues to be used as a storage facility. The use of timber from the farm in the construction of this barn illustrates once again the value of farm woodland. Approximately 80 percent of the lumber used in building the mule barn came from experiment station land. In addition to the lumber used in building the barn, there were seven thousand board feet of lumber sold from the farm's woodland in 1934. Receipts from the sale of timber and firewood cut on the farm's property that year totaled over $1,600.

In the spring of 1934, Chance applied to the Tennessee Emergency Relief Association for aid. Funding was provided, and a crew of men sponsored through the association was soon working at the station. They were to perform a variety of tasks on the farm, including the building of concrete bridges, the maintenance of roads and the construction of barns. In 1935, Chance began receiving aid from the Works Progress Administration and the Tennessee Valley Authority. The WPA was involved in the construction of houses and barns on the station, while the TVA worked on such problems as soil erosion and the feasibility of curing tobacco with air circulated by electricity.

The soil erosion project involved a topographical study by TVA engineers to determine the sites for settling tanks. Once the sites were selected, concrete tanks built by WPA workmen were placed. These tanks were periodically drained, and the soil caught was weighed and sampled. Various types of grass were grown above the tanks in hopes of finding a solution to the erosion problem facing area farmers. Funds for this project came exclusively from the TVA. The TVA was also involved in a project at the station directed at helping the tobacco farmer. This project dealt with the curing process of tobacco. With its electrification projects throughout Tennessee's rural areas being successful, the TVA wanted to show even more uses for electricity. In this vein, a barn equipped with electric fans was constructed on the experiment station. This barn, which also contained a furnace, was designed by TVA engineers and built with TVA funds. Its purpose was to provide for a controlled curing process that would produce a better-quality leaf and higher prices for the grower. The barn was used for a number of growing seasons, with results never being what was envisioned. The TVA barn was eventually stripped of all its electrical apparatus and used as a conventional curing barn.

While the government projects were beneficial both to the experiment station and to the local economy, their bureaucratic operation would often prove frustrating for Superintendent Chance. Correct filing of project proposals and the maintenance of precise records—even to the point of accountability for the loss of an iron wedge—were essential in gaining government aid. Following proper procedure, however, did not always guarantee success. With requests coming from so many quarters, the lack of funds made it impossible for Superintendent Chance to obtain the aid he requested. Despite temporary setbacks in his efforts to obtain government aid, Chance persevered, and the station continued to grow. The extent to which federal work programs helped in the early development of the Tobacco Experiment Station can still be seen today. By the end of 1938, six houses and seven barns had been built by workers from the various federal work programs on station property. Most of these buildings continue to be in use.

In addition to the improvements made by the federal agencies, the station grew in other ways. In 1935, the station acquired an additional 173 acres. This land, which had been foreclosed on by a local bank, was obtained through the Greene County Chancery Court for the sum of $7,850.00. An agreement between the county and the University of Tennessee saw the county paying half the cost of the land with the stipulation that it be used only for the purpose of agricultural research. Failure to comply with this agreement would result in the land becoming the property of Greene County. This new acreage was used to graze a herd of fifty white-faced heifers that the experiment station had acquired through the Drought Relief Agency. While the cattle did not cost anything, shipping costs amounted to $2.15 per head. The cattle had been shipped from the western section of the country and were reported to be in poor condition upon their arrival in Greeneville. Part of the agreement by which the cattle were acquired stated that they could not be sold for a period of two years.

At this time, the introduction of a beef cattle operation in east Tennessee was quite novel. Most farmers kept only a few milk cows to provide butter and milk for their families. The idea of raising cattle to be marketed for meat did not seem feasible to most east Tennessee farmers. Throughout the years, the work dealing with beef cattle at the Tobacco Experiment Station has helped revolutionize the cattle industry throughout the state. There also were some key additions to the station's personnel. On May 13, 1935, J.L. Vandiver came to work at the Tobacco Experiment Station in the position of assistant superintendent. Vandiver would become a valuable aid to Superintendent Chance, whose time was occupied in dealing with the red tape involved in gaining aid from the various federal programs. The station's tobacco breeding program was greatly benefited when Dr. C.C. Allison was hired through the United States Department of Agriculture. Allison was a plant pathologist, and his work laid the foundation for the breeding studies conducted by the experiment station. The breeding program was also aided during this period by the construction of a greenhouse in which studies could be conducted year round. As the decade of the 1930s drew to a close, the federal work programs began to be phased out. The nation's attention became focused on international affairs, and the effects of the Depression began to lessen. This held true for Greene County and the Tobacco Experiment Station as well. Young men left the farms for jobs in northern factories or to enlist in one of the armed services. The nation would soon be entering an era of dramatic social, economic and political change that would affect all areas of the nation's fabric, including the agricultural sector.

The need to clothe and feed a nation at war, coupled with advances in technology, led to an era of rapid growth in agriculture. The tobacco industry was affected by these changes, especially changes in social behavior. The war years saw more people smoking, especially women, than ever before. This increase in demand for tobacco would make the role of the Tobacco Experiment Station even more important to the tobacco farmer. During

Station employee Keith Effler cuts and spears burley on station grounds. *Photo by Chris Bickers.*

the first decade of the Tobacco Experiment Station's existence, the main emphasis had been placed on the establishment of the facility. Although experimental studies had been conducted during this period, no significant breakthroughs were reported. This continued during the war years. The station lost much of its manpower, and with the departure of Frank Chance in 1943, it also lost its sense of direction. The work at the station came almost to a standstill, and the need for a new impetus was great. This impetus was provided by the changes brought about by the Second World War. The need to produce more tobacco, and the technology that would make this possible, would set the stage for the station's work over the next twenty-five years.

Work conducted at the station during this period has probably had more of an impact on the tobacco industry than at any other time in the station's history. Advances in plant breeding and agronomics resulted in a number of major discoveries that have been beneficial to the farmer. Much of the station's success during this period can be attributed to a group of men who came to the station shortly after the Second World War. These men formed the nucleus of a workforce that remained nearly unchanged for the next thirty years. This continuity formed a workforce that was nearly family-like in its makeup. The quality and quantity of the work produced by this group of men reflects this closeness. The men who formed the backbone of this workforce were Wayland and Uel Wilhoit, Ogle Neas, Beryl Nichols, Bill Gosnell and Hugh Felts. Collectively, these men had over two hundred years of service to the Tobacco Experiment Station. The first of this group to be hired was Wayland Wilhoit, who started in 1932. Wayland replaced his father as farm foreman in 1937 and held that position until 1960, when he became a research technician with the USDA. He served in this capacity until his retirement in 1976. Uel Wilhoit worked at the station part time during his youth, and when he was discharged from the navy in 1946, he returned to continue the family tradition of farming. Uel became assistant foreman and then replaced Wayland as foreman when Wayland's position changed in 1960.

Upon Wayland's retirement in 1976, Uel took over his position with the USDA and remained there until his retirement in 1989. Bill Gosnell came to the experiment station shortly after his return home from the war. "Uncle Bill," as he came to be called, had been reared in a section of Greene County known as Kitchen Creek. This area was noted for the toughness of its inhabitants and its number of moonshine stills per capita. His background had served Gosnell well on the battlefields of Europe, and when he came to the station, he was ready for anything. Although he possessed only a third grade education, Gosnell gained a reputation throughout the university's

Right: In Greeneville, Tennessee, a worker at the Tobacco Research Station pushes burley tobacco stalks onto a pointed metal cone. The stalks slip over the "spear" and hang from the stick it is balanced on. *Photo by Chris Bickers.*

Below: Stalks hang from sticks in Weaverville, North Carolina.*Photo by Chris Bickers.*

agricultural system for his abilities in all areas of farming. In fact, there was more than one instance in which the man with the third grade education gave lessons to some of the college professors. Gosnell became farm foreman in 1976 and served in that position until his retirement in 1988.

93

Spearing burley stalks in Buncombe County, North Carolina. *Photo by Chris Bickers.*

The three men mentioned above formed a triumvirate that provided the station with steady leadership for over thirty years. Wayland Wilhoit supervised the station's tobacco operation; Uel Wilhoit oversaw the station's cattle and forage crops; and Gosnell was responsible for the maintenance of the farm's machinery. With these three men leading the day-to-day work of the station, the superintendent was free to focus on other administrative duties.

Ogle Neas began his career at the Tobacco Experiment Station in September 1943. Neas, a native Greene Countian, had been teaching high school industrial arts prior to coming to the station. He was hired through the USDA to assist in the station's tobacco breeding program. Although possessing no formal training in genetics or plant pathology, Neas quickly picked up on the art of plant breeding. A penchant for detail coupled with an uncanny eye for plant selection would make him one of the most successful tobacco breeders of all time. In a career that spanned more than thirty years, Neas was involved in the development and release of nine superior varieties of burley tobacco. Beryl Nichols, reared on a farm in Knox County and a graduate of the University of Tennessee, was hired through the USDA as station agronomist in 1948. Prior to his employment with the station, he had been mapping soil types throughout east Tennessee. As station agronomist, Nichols was involved in a variety of experiments dealing with all phases of agronomics. His most prominent work was in the areas of soil fertility and tobacco growth regulators. In over thirty years of service, "Nick," as he was known to most, was involved in a number of organizations associated with the tobacco industry. Among these organizations were the Tobacco Workers Conference, the Tobacco Growth Regulator Committee and the Tobacco Chemists Conference.

The catalyst of this group of men was Hugh Felts. Felts became station superintendent in 1946, replacing interim superintendent J.L. Vandiver. Felts, a native of Robertson County, Tennessee, and a graduate of the University of Tennessee, had served as the director of 4-H clubs in both Greene and Washington Counties and was a former county agent. During the war, Felts worked for the Emergency Farm Labor Program. In this capacity, Felts organized labor for projects such as the harvesting of the bean crop in Johnson County, Tennessee, and of the Idaho potato crop. Following the war, Felts was offered the job of station superintendent by fellow Robertson Countian Frank Chance, who was the assistant director of all the university's experiment stations. Felts served as the Tobacco Experiment Station's superintendent until he retired in 1974.

While this group of men was to a large extent responsible for the excellent work produced by

Top: Burley hangs in a barn near Asheville, North Carolina. *Photo by Chris Bickers.*

Right: A harvest worker sharpens his tobacco knife while harvesting burley near Boone, North Carolina. *Photo by Chris Bickers.*

the station during this period, there were many others involved. The USDA was heavily involved in the work at the station. Dr. H.E. Heggestad, H.A. Skoog, Robert Davis, Dr. Loren J. Hoffbeck, Dr. R.C. Sievert and Dr. C.L. Gupton were among those who worked at the station. Their work in the areas of plant breeding and agronomy was critical to the success of the station. In discussing the personnel involved in the growth of the Tobacco Experiment Station, the field men, who did the actual work required in the various experiments conducted at the station, were most important. Their dedication carried them through the heat of summer and the chill of winter. It led them to persevere, even though some of the tasks they were asked to perform seemed unnecessary and fruitless. These men who raised their families in houses owned by the station and whose sons replaced them after they retired are a major reason for the station's success. It is families such as the Henry Davises, the Willie Riddles and the Luke Justices that remain the bedrock of the Tobacco Experiment Station.

The station's personnel found themselves increasingly busier as the station grew. By 1955, the station acreage had grown to over 530 acres. This land was purchased from the neighboring farms of Beverly Williams, G.R. Wilhoit, Silas Wills and O.C. Mays. Much of this new acreage was in poor shape, and many man-hours were used in getting the land into production. The station's physical growth was also aided by the addition of a number of buildings. Between 1945 and 1965, there were thirteen new structures constructed on the station. Of these structures, there were five houses, three tobacco barns, two cattle barns, a farm shop, a greenhouse and an administration building. Most of these buildings were constructed by the station's crew in addition to its maintaining normal farm operations. The construction of a second greenhouse was deemed most essential because of the growth of the station's breeding program. The hard work and dedication of the station's plant breeders culminated in the release of seven new varieties of burley tobacco between 1950 and 1965. The first variety of tobacco to be released by the station was given the name Burley 1. This variety, released in 1950, was the answer to the black root rot problem that had plagued growers for years. Burley 1 was highly resistant to black root rot and still maintained the high quality required by the tobacco companies.

In 1952, the station released Burley 2. This variety, a sister line of Burley 1, had similar characteristics. It, too, was highly resistant to black root rot and was cited as having good quality and high yield. The station released two varieties of tobacco in 1954. Designated Burley 11A and Burley 11B, these two varieties were a major breakthrough because of their resistance to black shank and

Fusarium wilt disease. As with Burley 1 and Burley 2, these varieties were also resistant to black root rot, making them even more valuable to the grower. The need for a variety of tobacco resistant to black shank was essential due to the high level of destruction caused by this disease.

This soil-borne disease first appeared on east Tennessee farms in the late 1940s and attacks a tobacco plant through its root system, eventually working its way into the stalk. Early symptoms are wilted leaves in the heat of the day; the leaves closest to the ground turn a bright yellow and then wither and turn brown as the disease progresses. The shank of the plant turns black, and the inside of the stalk becomes hollow. Depending on the severity of black shank present in a field, losses can range as high as 100 percent. The most difficult problem in dealing with black shank is its easy transmittal. The disease can be brought into a field through flooding or on equipment that has been used in a contaminated field and not sterilized or on the feet of humans and animals. As with black root rot, black shank multiplies each year that tobacco is grown in contaminated soil. Because of this, growers had to rely on crop rotation to fight the disease. With the introduction of Burley 11A and 11B, tobacco growers were able to utilize land that had previously been unsuitable for tobacco cultivation because of the presence of black shank. However, growers were reminded that these new varieties were resistant, not immune, to black shank and that some form of crop rotation should be followed to prevent a buildup of the disease.

The release of Burley 21 in 1955 is probably the greatest achievement of the Tobacco Experiment Station's breeding program. This variety was the first tobacco of any type to be resistant to the serious bacterial disease wildfire. Tobacco plants infected with wildfire can be identified by dark-colored lesions on the leaves. Within a few days of the appearance of these lesions, a pale yellow halo will appear around each lesion. Under conditions of high moisture, the disease may appear as a wet rot, causing the collapse of entire lower leaves and even the death of small seedlings. Established transplants usually survive an attack by wildfire but with a reduction in quality and yield. The disease is most destructive in seedbeds where the bacterial toxins enter the vascular systems of the seedlings. Once the disease infests a plant bed, there is usually a 100 percent loss.

In addition to wildfire resistance, Burley 21 was also resistant to tobacco mosaic virus and black root rot. The development of this variety took nearly twenty years with the hundreds of crosses involved in its background, illustrating the time-consuming effort required in the development of a new variety of tobacco. The release of Burley 21 was a cumulative effort between the USDA and various agricultural experiment facilities throughout the tobacco-producing states. The work began in 1938, when Dr. E.E. Clayton of the USDA's Beltsville, Maryland Experiment Station developed a hybrid between the two wild species *N. macumba* and *N. longiflora*. The work continued throughout the next two decades, with M.O. Neas and H.E. Heggestad of the University of Tennessee's Tobacco Experiment Station playing a vital role in its final development. Tobacco growers throughout the world owe a debt of gratitude to those involved in the development of Burley 21 because before its inception, wildfire threatened the entire tobacco industry. Reports from 1948 indicated that wildfire was present in at least 75 percent of the burley fields in eastern Tennessee and that the outbreak in Kentucky was the most extensive in thirty years. In some counties, the disease was so rampant that the growing of tobacco was nearly impossible. In the years since the release of Burley 21, there have been a number of new varieties of tobacco developed. Most of these varieties produce tobacco that is of better quality and also has greater yields than Burley 21. Although the new varieties may be superior to Burley 21 in these areas, nearly all of the new varieties have Burley 21 in their pedigree because of the need for wildfire resistance.

In 1960, the station released Burley 37. This variety, resistant to black shank and wildfire, also had moderate resistance to black root rot and Fusarium wilt. Burley 37 was a cross between Burley 21 and Burley 11A. This gave the new variety resistance to black shank, which Burley 21 did not have, and to wildfire, which Burley 11A did not possess. This new variety was comparable to other varieties in yield and quality and was highly recommended to growers where black shank was prevalent. Burley 49, released to growers in 1965, gave growers the same resistance to black shank and wildfire as Burley 37 but with a higher resistance to black root rot. This variety was also moderately resistant to tobacco mosaic virus and Fusarium wilt disease. As with most of the other varieties developed at the station, Burley 49 was a stand-up type of tobacco. This meant that the leaves of the plant tended to stand up rather than droop over, as in the case of many older varieties. This characteristic allowed for tasks such as topping and suckering to be accomplished without as much damage to the leaves. Quality and yield of Burley 49 was about the same as Burley 37; however, Burley 49's stalk was smaller than Burley 37's, making for easier handling at harvest.

Most of the varieties mentioned here are no longer popular with growers. They have been replaced by varieties that combine resistance to an array of diseases with the potential for enormous yields. However, most of these new varieties, whether hybrids released through seed companies or new varieties achieved through selective breeding, have somewhere in their lineage one or more of the varieties developed at the station. The station's breeding program was, and still is, a very important aspect of the station's mission. The need to develop new varieties of tobacco is constant because of the influx of new disease or a new strain of an old one. Important as the station's breeding program may be, it is not the only work conducted at the station. The development of ways to help the farmer produce larger yields with less effort is another important part of the station's work. Studies dealing with such agronomic practices as soil fertility, irrigation, sucker control, plant bed practices, dates of harvest and plant spacing were aimed at helping the farmer improve his situation.

When station agronomist B.C. Nichols began his career in 1948, he was told by his superiors that they wanted to show farmers how to increase tobacco yields through the use of commercial fertilizer. Tobacco growers had traditionally been reluctant to use sizable amounts of fertilizer on their tobacco for fear of hurting the quality of the leaf. While it was true that too much nitrogen would produce a dark, heavy-bodied leaf that was too harsh for cigarettes, Nichols felt that there was a middle ground where increased yields and acceptable quality could both be found. Nichols initiated tests involving previously unheard of rates of fertilizer, using various rates ranging from extremes in high and low amounts. A variety of cover crops and varying rates of manure were also included as part of the experimental program. The study was conducted over a number of growing seasons with results being compiled concerning areas such as yield, quality and chemical analysis. This study revealed that the rate of nitrogen used on tobacco could be tripled from what was previously thought acceptable without harming the quality of the tobacco. This work in fertility was largely responsible for an increase in tobacco yields in Tennessee from 900 pounds per acre before the Second World War to nearly 1,800 pounds per acre by 1958.

The problem of sucker control was another area into which the station has put a great deal of effort. Tobacco growers spent countless hours in their fields removing these troublesome offshoots that grew from the plant's main stalk at the point where the leaves are attached. These suckers had to be removed because they robbed the main plant of the nutrients it needed to grow and mature properly. Before the release of sucker control agents, a tobacco crop had to be suckered several times before harvest. With the advent of sucker controls, the farmer has to sucker his tobacco only at topping time and then spray the plant with the chemical to inhibit further sucker growth. Hundreds of chemicals were tested in an effort to find an effective means of halting sucker growth without harming the tobacco. A committee known as the Tobacco Growth Regulator Committee was formed to oversee and review the results of the testing of these chemicals. A number of chemicals that looked promising in the field because of their effectiveness in halting sucker growth were eliminated following chemical analysis of the tobacco on which they had been used. Other chemicals were eliminated because they reduced the filling value of the tobacco, making them economically unsuitable to the tobacco companies. Several of the chemicals passed the field tests, the quality tests and the chemical analysis only to be failed by a taste test. The stringent requirements set forth by the Growth Regulator Committee were meant to safeguard the tobacco industry from charges by anti-smoking groups of negligence in the use of chemicals on tobacco. Because of this strict enforcement, a sucker control agent was not released until the late 1960s.

From 1955 until 1963, the station did a study on the feasibility of using irrigation on tobacco. Varying amounts of water coupled with several rates of nitrogen were used in this test. Results were kept on yield, quality and chemical analysis. It was finally determined that the cost of an irrigation system was not feasible for most tobacco growers because of the fact that, due to the average amount of annual rainfall in this region, the system would be used only one year in ten.

Tests involving topping heights and time of harvest were conducted in order to find the optimum height at which to top the tobacco and the proper interval between topping and harvest. This was done in order to maximize quality and yield. These tests were especially important in the era before sucker controls because if the farmer topped too early, he would have to sucker his crop again while waiting for it to ripen. Also if he waited too long, especially in a dry season, he would begin losing the bottom leaves, which ripen and dry up first. Records were kept on yield, quality and chemical composition, with the results being used to determine the practices that would prove most beneficial to the grower. Various topping heights were used in an effort to find the optimum height for quality leaf production. Dates of harvest after topping ranged from as few as one week to as many as six weeks. Studies dealing with plant bed practices were another important project undertaken by the station. Tests involving soil fertility, control of diseases and insects were all vital; however, the greatest achievement to come from this work was the use of methyl bromide gas for weed control. Before the advent of this gas, the tobacco farmer spent a great deal of time hauling and burning brush on his plant beds to eliminate weeds. With the methyl bromide gas, all the farmer has to do is release the gas under a plastic cover that has been placed over the bed and secured around the edges with dirt. This method is not only much faster but also more effective, with little or no weeding required afterward. Although methyl bromide was not invented by the station, the tests conducted there helped to get it approved for release to the public and helped it gain public acceptance once it was released. Many of the cultural practices and chemical aids used by today's tobacco grower are the result of the agronomic work conducted by the station. As with all other work at the station, these studies were a cooperative effort between the personnel of the Tobacco Experiment Station, the University of Tennessee and the USDA. Their commitment is reflected in the quality of the work performed during this period.

Mechanization came to the station in the early 1950s. Tractors took the place of horses and mules, paving the way for a new era in the station's history. Modern machinery powered by the tractors' live power systems made the old horse-drawn equipment obsolete. This new equipment made tasks such as plowing, mowing hay and combining wheat much faster than had previously been possible. The piece of equipment that probably had the greatest impact on the tobacco grower was the mechanical transplanter. The mechanical transplanter, or setter, makes a furrow, places a plant in the furrow, waters the plant and then firms the soil up around the plant. Two people ride the setter, alternately placing plants in the setter's revolving pockets as it is pulled through the field by a tractor. The mechanical transplanter is not only much faster than previous methods of setting tobacco, but it also allows for precise watering and spacing of plants. The mechanical transplanter was originally designed to plant strawberries on large commercial farms.

Bill Gosnell saw a photograph of a transplanter in an agricultural magazine and became convinced that it would work with tobacco. Gosnell brought this to Hugh Felts's attention, and Felts agreed with the assessment. Felts contacted a local farm equipment dealer and asked him to obtain a transplanter. The dealer had one shipped to the station, and the setter was unveiled before the public early one spring at a plant bed demonstration. Since it was too early in the season to have plants large enough to set, Felts had his men break sprigs off bushes to approximate the size of a tobacco plant. The crowd was brought to a field that had been prepared for the demonstration, and the setter was put to work. The transplanter was an instant hit, and the equipment dealer, who just happened to be in attendance, left that afternoon with nearly one hundred orders for the transplanters. The mechanical transplanter revolutionized the tobacco industry. The amount of labor saved coupled with increased survival rates of transplants has enabled growers to expand their operations and reduce the amount of time spent on the crop at the same time. The role of the experiment station in bringing the mechanical transplanter into use by tobacco growers is an example of how the station has helped growers. It also illustrates the innovativeness and downright common sense of the station's personnel.

This type of creative thinking has helped solve myriad problems throughout the station's history. Work in areas other than that related to tobacco production expanded during this period. The station's beef cattle operation grew, gaining wide acclaim for its work in breeding and nutrition. Testing of a variety of small grain and forage crops was essential in the development of new varieties for the farmer. The station also conducted tests dealing with the feasibility of raising sheep in east Tennessee and the phenomena of dwarfism in cattle. No matter what the project, the ultimate aim of the station is to find something that will aid the farmer. The primary reason for the station's existence is for the benefit of the farmer, and it is toward this goal that the station must strive.

This belief has run into opposition from time to time from people who are distrustful of anything connected with the government. This is especially true of the older generation of farmers who, for the most part, are of an independent nature. People of this nature are often reluctant to change because of the tenacity of tradition. The battle against this type of thinking has faced the experiment station from its inception. An example of the difficulty the station has faced in trying to gain acceptance from some farmers is found in a story about a farmer in middle Tennessee. This older farmer had grown a crop of the then new variety Burley 11B. About the midpoint of the growing season, the farmer contacted the station to complain about the fact that the black shank–resistant variety was dying in his field. When representatives of the station investigated, they found that less than 1 percent of his crop was infested by black shank. Upon further inquiry, they learned that the farmer had absorbed a 90 percent loss of his crop the previous year when he grew the variety Kentucky 16. The farmer related that he had grown tobacco in this particular piece of ground for seventeen years even though he had plenty of other land available to use for crop rotation. The reason given for continued use was that the field was in proximity to his barn and that this field is where he had always grown his tobacco. When it was pointed out to the man that he was going to be over 90 percent better off by raising Burley 11B than he had been previously, he still remained adamant about the fact that the new variety was not what it was reported to be even though the variety was listed as being resistant, not immune, to black shank.

This example, although somewhat extreme, does reveal the fact that the station's work and materials are not accepted by everyone. A number of tactics were used to try to rectify this situation, including the publication of reports and bulletins that detailed the station's work. The station's annual Field Days were also used to gain public support for the work being conducted there. The success of these events continued throughout the 1950s and 1960s. Crowds numbering in the hundreds came out to the station to see firsthand the various experiments being conducted there. The station hosted a number of dignitaries such as state and national legislators and commissioners of agriculture during these Field Days. The 1959 Field Day was noted as being special because of the attendance of former superintendent Frank Chance. The reunion between the retired Chance and some of his former employees was an emotional scene. Especially poignant was the meeting between Chance and Mrs. Bessie Wilhoit, widow of F.C. Wilhoit and co-owner with her husband of the original tract sold to the university. Clyde Austin, one of the originators of the station and probably its greatest supporter throughout the early years, was on hand to welcome Chance back to Greene County. Nearly one thousand farmers were in attendance for this Field Day, which featured a presentation by Dr. J.E. McMurtrey, head of the USDA's tobacco research program, outlining the history of the station's tobacco breeding program. Comments from local farmers in attendance were favorable in regard to the station's work. The development of improved varieties of tobacco was especially noted as being helpful to the farmer.

The efforts of the Tobacco Experiment Station to develop ways by which the tobacco farmer could improve his lot began paying dividends. Records show a steady improvement in tobacco yields throughout the burley tobacco belt. In Tennessee, the averages went from slightly over 1,000 pounds per acre in 1940 to over 1,900 pounds per acre in 1965. Prices paid for the tobacco rose steadily as well, from a little over eighteen cents a pound in 1940 to over sixty-nine cents a pound in 1965. This added up to an improvement in the way of life for the tobacco farmer. The period between the end of the Second World War and the early 1960s will probably come to be viewed as the Golden Age of the tobacco industry. Increased domestic consumption coupled with an expanded foreign market, made possible by the destruction of Britain's colonial tobacco industry, resulted in a tremendous increase in the demand for U.S. tobacco. This created a boom that affected every sector of the tobacco industry from the tobacco companies to the small-time grower. This boom period was soon threatened by a number of factors. Among these factors were the increased pressure from health groups concerning the link between smoking and health problems, renewed competition from foreign tobacco markets and increased production costs for growers.

Finding ways to overcome these problems required much time and effort. The Tobacco Experiment Station continued to lead the way in the search for solutions to these and many other problems confronting the tobacco grower. In 1964, the U.S. surgeon general concluded in his landmark report, "Smoking and Health," that cigarettes are a health hazard. This finding prompted a series of studies and the implementation of many regulations that have permanently altered the Western world's perception of tobacco. The most dramatic indication of smoker concern is the rising popularity of low-tar cigarettes. The change from filterless cigarettes to the filtered low-tar version enabled cigarette manufacturers to use lower-quality tobacco in their product. This trend has resulted in an increased use of foreign tobacco in the manufacture of cigarettes. Expanding tobacco production in Africa, Asia and Latin America now poses a serious threat to continued American dominance of the world leaf market. Foreign tobacco, with nearly the same quality of domestic tobacco, can be bought at one-third to one-half the cost of domestic tobacco. In addition to the threats presented by the health concerns and foreign competition, the American tobacco grower has found himself beset by inflation, high energy and fertilizer prices and rising labor costs. The combination of these factors has led to troubled times for the American tobacco grower. Attempts to reverse the fortunes of the U.S. tobacco industry have been made from several quarters. Most notable in this effort has been the advertising and lobbying sponsored by U.S. tobacco companies aimed at the claims laid by anti-tobacco groups. In addition, the tobacco companies have spent millions of dollars on the development of foreign markets for American-made cigarettes.

Government control of the U.S. tobacco market has also helped American tobacco farmers compete in the world market. Governmental regulation in tobacco began in 1938 with the Second Agricultural Adjustment Act. Under this program, the tobacco grower was allowed a basic quota of tobacco that he could sell in a particular year. Participants in the program were eligible for government-sponsored price supports. The overall purpose of this program was to stabilize prices by restricting supply. Prior to 1971, tobacco quotas were allotted in terms of acreage; each grower was allowed to grow a specific amount of tobacco acreage on his farm. A lease and transfer program allowed one allotment holder to lease quotas from others in the same county for production on his farm. In 1971, the quota system was changed to a poundage allocation. Advantages of this system were that it allowed the grower to over market by 10 percent and to carry over to the following season any poundage he failed to have the previous year. This system maintained the lease and transfer program and helped strengthen the tobacco market. In this marketing system, any tobacco not purchased by the tobacco companies was bought by stabilization cooperatives at a set government-support price. The tobacco purchased by these cooperatives was processed and stored for later sale to the tobacco companies. The money to purchase, process and store the tobacco is borrowed from the Commodity Credit Corporation, a USDA lending agency. The use of taxpayers' money to support this program came under attack from the anti-smoking groups, and in 1985, a change was made in the way the program was conducted. The grower assumed responsibility for the administrative costs of running the program. These costs included processing, storage, handling and the payment of interest on the CCC loan. The new program also called for a reduction in price supports in order to make domestic tobacco more competitive in the world market.

Throughout these changing and often turbulent times, the Tobacco Experiment Station has continued its mission of helping the farmer. In response to the economic pressures confronting tobacco growers, the station began to direct its attention toward studies dealing with reducing the costs involved in raising tobacco. The station's tobacco-breeding program also continued in its effort to develop varieties of tobacco that can be of benefit to the grower. Since 1968, the station has been involved in the development of three new varieties of burley tobacco—with a fourth variety that was under consideration for release in 1991. The station has also played a major role in the testing of a variety of chemicals developed to aid the farmer. Herbicides such as 2, 4-D, Prowl and Enide; the insecticides Orthene, Furadan and Lorsban; and the sucker control agents MH-30 and Prime + have all been tested at the station prior to their release to the public. The station's physical growth has also continued. Since 1965, the station has added a large utility building, three tobacco barns, a chemical storage building and a large metal building that serves as a combination shop and tractor shed.

A great deal of renovation work has also been performed on the station's houses and the administration building. The most versatile of these structures is the utility building. Constructed in 1966, this 118- by 32-foot building serves as a storage facility for a variety of tools and other equipment and as a meeting place for the station's crew. It is also the location in which the station's tobacco is stripped and prepared for market. Four large rooms in the basement of this building provide a warm, well-lit place in which the station's crew grades the farm's tobacco for market. The station's annual tobacco show also takes place in the basement of this utility building. The show brings representatives from all the major tobacco companies to view tobacco brought in from all the burley-producing states. The tobacco is rated by the representatives for its quality and usefulness to the tobacco companies. This tobacco show gives researchers an opportunity to find out if their experimental work can be of practical use.

There have been no additional land acquisitions by the station since the early 1950s. As a matter of fact, the station's size has been slightly reduced by the sale of twenty-five acres to the Town of Greeneville for the purpose of constructing a sewage treatment plant. The station has periodically entered into lease agreements to gain additional cropland; this practice will continue with the lease of the 150-acre Austin farm beginning in 1990. This land will give the station additional acreage to be utilized for plot work.

One of the biggest changes that have occurred at the station within the past twenty years has been in the area of personnel. Beginning in the mid-1970s with the retirements of Hugh Felts, Ogle Neas and Wayland Wilhoit, the station began to see a change in the old guard that had been a steadying force since the mid-1940s. Cutbacks in federal funding resulted in the withdrawal of the majority of the USDA personnel by the late 1970s. By the early 1980s, the only federal funding coming into the experiment station was for the salaries of Beryl Nichols and Uel Wilhoit, and with the retirement of Nichols in 1981 and of Wilhoit in 1989, this funding ceased. The withdrawal by the federal government from the station ended a relationship of nearly sixty years. The reasons for this pullout vary from economic factors to political pressure from health groups, but whatever the reason, the reality is that the full responsibility for the station's continuance is now in the hands of the State of Tennessee. In addition to those mentioned above, the station has lost a number of longtime members of its farm crew. Bill Gosnell was forced into retirement in 1988 due to health reasons, leaving a huge void in the crew's makeup. Other longtime employees who have retired during this period include Henry Davis, Luke Justice, Donald Stone, Horace Effler, Willie Riddle, Herman Riddle, Roy Brank, John Barner and Tom Cutshaw. These men were involved in some of the most vital work ever conducted at the station, with much of the station's success being owed to their hard work and dedication.

Of course, change is an ever present fact of life, with the need to infuse new blood into the system being necessary for continued growth. An assessment of how the new generation at the Tobacco Experiment Station will fare in comparison with the old crew cannot be made at this point because of the difference in time on the job between the two groups. A major problem that faces the present crew is a lack of continuity. With higher-paying jobs available in Greene County's ever-growing industrial base, people today must weigh some of the esoteric advantages of farming against financial considerations. This has resulted in a workforce that is not as stable as it was in previous times.

The station's leadership has also seen changes in the past fifteen years. In 1974, Dr. Donald Howard replaced Hugh Felts as station superintendent.

Howard, a native of Oklahoma, earned a PhD in soil chemistry from Auburn University and served as a soil fertility specialist in Tennessee's Agricultural Extension Service before coming to the station. Under Howard's leadership, the station undertook such projects as fly control with beef cattle, insect control and labor studies in tobacco, variety trials and herbicide tests in soybeans and no-till production in corn and alfalfa. Results of these and other projects were presented to extension leaders during in-service training sessions conducted by Howard. The extension personnel would in turn inform farmers in their various locales of the new information. Howard cites the upgrading of the station's facilities and equipment as being the major accomplishment during his tenure at the station. A major renovation of the station's on-farm housing was accomplished without an increase in budget. In addition to this work, the station's crew constructed one burley barn and made improvements on several other barns. They also built a large equipment storage shed and a cattle-handling facility comprising five holding pens with a set of scales and a head gate under the roof. Efforts at keeping the station's equipment updated included the purchase of a John Deere hay baler that had an attachment that kicked the hay bales into an enclosed wagon being pulled behind the baler. By using this system, one man could handle the entire operation of harvesting the farm's hay. Howard also tried to update the station's tractor fleet. When he came to the station in 1974, the newest tractor in inventory was seven years old. Upon his departure in 1981, the oldest tractor at the station was seven years old. Strained relations between Howard, USDA personnel, university staff and various community leaders in Greene County led to his departure. He was reassigned to the university's West Tennessee Experiment Station in Jackson, Tennessee, to conduct studies in soil fertility.

In July 1981, Dr. Phil Hunter became superintendent of the Tobacco Experiment Station. Hunter, whose father was a longtime county extension agent in Greene County, graduated from Greeneville High School and the University of Tennessee and received his PhD from Virginia Polytechnic Institute. Prior to coming to the experiment station, Hunter had been working at the University of Tennessee's Highland Rim Experiment Station at Springfield. His position there was partly extension work with area farmers and partly research work dealing with dark fired and dark air-cured tobacco.

When Hunter first arrived at the station, he found that most of the research being conducted was in the area of agronomics. Feeling that the research in this area had gone as far as it could—farmers already knew the optimum rates of fertility, the best types of cover crop and the best types of weed control—Hunter began to focus on the economic side of tobacco farming. Together with researchers such as Dr. Darrel Mundy and Dr. Zak Henry from the university's main campus, the station undertook studies dealing with the areas of cost and labor. Financial difficulties have plagued the station just as they have many tobacco growers in the past decade. Budget reductions and withdrawal of federal money have made an impact on the station's operations. To counteract this financial deficit, the station has had to rely heavily on the sale of tobacco during Hunter's tenure. The station's income is also aided through research grants given out by tobacco companies. In 1989, the station's tobacco-breeding program generated over $100,000 worth of revenue for the station through research grants.

In Hunter's assessment of what the most important thing the station has done to help the farmer since his arrival, he points to two things. The first of these is the development and release of the tobacco variety Tennessee 86, and the second is the work that the station has done in reducing costs and labor for the tobacco grower. Another area that needed help when Hunter arrived was the station's tobacco-breeding program. With the retirement of Ogle Neas in 1974 and the pullout of most of the USDA personnel in the late 1970s, the station's breeding program had gone into a decline. The station had not released a variety of tobacco since Burley 64 in 1973, and there was no new work being conducted at the station when Hunter arrived. To correct this problem, the university hired Dr. Robert Miller as the station's tobacco breeder in 1982.

Miller grew up on a tobacco farm near London, Kentucky, and is a graduate of Berea College and the University of Kentucky, where he received his PhD in plant and soil sciences. Miller had been working as a dark tobacco breeder for the University of Kentucky before coming to the station. Although the position of tobacco breeder had been vacant for nearly three years, Miller found that the material left by the former breeder, Dr. C.L. Gupton, showed much promise. Miller began working with some of the lines left by Gupton that showed resistance to the potato virus Y complex (PVY). This virus, along with tobacco vein mottling virus (TVMV) and tobacco etch virus (TEV), was becoming widespread throughout the burley-producing states in the early 1980s. These viruses are transmitted by green peach aphids and can be found in almost all fields of tobacco in east Tennessee and Kentucky. Initial symptoms of these diseases may be limited to a slight mottling or yellowing of the tissue around the veins of the leaves. As the disease progresses, leaf speckling and necrosis may result in leaf deterioration. This often causes premature harvesting of the tobacco, resulting in reduced yield and quality.

Flowers hold the promise of a big burley crop at the Greeneville station.

Attempts to develop a variety of burley tobacco that was resistant to these viruses had failed because the primary source of tobacco used to incorporate virus resistance did not produce the trichome exudates (tobacco gum) normally found on most tobacco varieties. The crosses that were made with this primary source—known as Virgin A Mutant—had good resistance to the viruses; however, the smooth, non-secreting leaves were highly susceptible to insect damage. Miller found that some of the lines left by Gupton had normal secretions as well as virus resistance. These lines were crossed with varieties known for their overall disease resistance as well as for quality and yield. After four years of selective breeding and testing, a new variety was released. This new variety, designated Tennessee 86 (TN86), was released to growers in 1986. This variety is the only burley tobacco variety in the world to have resistance to tobacco etch virus, tobacco vein mottling virus and potato virus Y. In addition, TN86 is also resistant to black shank, black root rot and wildfire. Like most of the varieties developed at the station, TN86 is a standup type of tobacco. It produces more leaves than most other burley varieties and has a medium-size stalk diameter. In terms of yield and quality, TN86 rates favorably with the highest yielding commercial varieties and received the highest ratings in industry evaluations for leaf color, quality and usability.

As of the 1989 growing season, TN86 was ranked sixth in popularity among burley tobacco growers. Its failure to gain a wider acceptance is due to a number of factors. First, TN86 has no resistance to tobacco mosaic virus. Second, it has had trouble making inroads into the large Kentucky market because of the popularity of the hybrid variety KY14XL8 in that state. Third, TN86 is a late maturing variety, the yield of which is cut drastically by early harvest. Last, and most significant, is the fact that during the first three years in which TN86 was available to the public, the tobacco-growing states were experiencing one of the most extensive droughts in their history. The late maturing TN86 suffered more loss in yield than did some of the other burley varieties in these drought conditions, and many growers lost confidence in the variety.

Because of the shortcomings that growers have found in TN86, the station's tobacco-breeding program continued to search for a virus-resistant variety that would be more attractive to the grower. This search culminated in the development of a breeding line designated Greeneville 141 (GR141), which has resistance to tobacco mosaic virus as well as the other viruses that TN86 has resistance against. This new variety is an earlier maturing tobacco than TN86, and it also has a smaller diameter stalk than TN86. In tests conducted at the station, and on a number of farms throughout east Tennessee, this new variety has compared favorably with TN86 in both yield and quality. Released in 1990, the variety was designated Tennessee 90 (TN90).

The development and release of new varieties of tobacco such as TN86 and TN90 is what the station's tobacco-breeding program has always been about. Unlike commercial seed companies that make hybrid crosses between popular varieties as a marketing ploy, the station's breeding program does not seek to release a variety unless it is superior in some way to anything else available to the grower. This tradition is being carried on in today's tobacco-breeding program. The varieties of tobacco developed at the experiment station in recent years combine resistance to as many as seven diseases with yields of nearly three thousand pounds per acre. The station releases these new varieties to the public freely, receiving no monetary compensation. The impact of the tobacco varieties developed at the Tobacco Experiment Station on the tobacco industry has been enormous. The money that Burley 21 alone has saved the tobacco industry would probably have been enough to pay for the station's operation throughout its history.

In addition to the success of the station's tobacco-breeding program, a number of advancements have been made in other areas of the station's research program. Efforts aimed at cutting labor and production costs began at the station in the mid-1970s. Among the early efforts:

* *"Priming" of burley leaf followed by curing in flue-cured-style bulk barns.* This priming, which is widely used in flue-cured tobacco, involves taking the leaves off the stalks as they ripen in the field and placing them in baskets, which are taken to special curing barns. The baskets of leaves are placed in the bulk-curing barns, and the curing process, which uses artificial heat, begins. This effort, unfortunately, was not a success. Researchers at the station hoped that the initial costs of this system would be offset by the labor saved. However, as it turned out, the quality found in traditionally air-cured burley tobacco could not be attained through this process.

* *Market preparation/sheeting.* This study was done in response to changes in the tobacco market that opened the way for sale of loose-leaf tobacco. When the tobacco companies opened the way for loose-leaf marketing, the first method devised was known as "sheeting." In this procedure, the tobacco was placed on burlap sheets. The leaves were loosely placed in a circle, with the stems pointing toward the outside of the circle. When the desired amount of tobacco had been placed on the sheet, the corners were brought together and tied. This method of preparing tobacco for market eliminated

the time-consuming process of tying and packing hands of tobacco. However, the bulky sheets of loose tobacco created handling problems for the warehousemen and tobacco companies. This method was never widely used and was eventually phased out of the marketing system.

* *Market preparation/baling.* The next step toward marketing loose-leaf tobacco was baling the leaves. Studies conducted initially at the University of Kentucky had revealed the promise that lay in this process of preparing tobacco for market. These studies, along with some conducted in the University of Tennessee's Department of Agricultural Economics and Rural Sociology, led to a trial marketing of baled tobacco in 1978. In this trial year, each county was allowed to sell 15 percent of its basic tobacco quota in bales. Farmers were reluctant to switch to this new method out of fear that the tobacco companies would not pay the same price for baled tobacco as for hand-tied. In the early years of baling, this was true, for baled tobacco brought around five cents per pound less than hand-tied tobacco. But as word circulated among growers relating the advantages of baling versus hand-tied, more tobacco companies were forced to accept the change. There is no mystery why. Labor studies conducted at the experiment station by Darrel Mundy concluded that baling reduces the amount of time spent in the marketing process by nearly one-third. The use of the tobacco baler is probably second only to the mechanical transplanter in its impact on cutting the amount of time involved in tobacco production.

* *Plant populations.* Prior to 1971, when the quota system changed from acreage to poundage, growers spaced their tobacco as close together as was deemed possible within the farmer's allotted acreage. The theory behind this was that the more plants grown per acre, the more pounds that acre would produce. While it is true that dense plant populations will out yield lower plant populations if properly fertilized, one must also look at the extra labor involved in handling the higher number of plants. Research, therefore, began to focus on finding the optimum plant spacing that would combine good yield with a reduced amount of labor. Although the station had conducted work involving plant spacing in the 1960s and 1970s, the emphasis placed on it was not great. Since then, however, factors such as rising production costs and labor shortages have caused a shift in emphasis toward this area.

In the mid-1980s, Darrel Mundy and research associate Steve Isaacs began extensive research into the relationship between plant populations and labor costs. In their studies, a variety of plant spacings were used, ranging from twelve-inch in-row by thirty-six-inch between-row to one-inch in-row by fifty-four-inch between-row spacing. In using this wide range of spacings, they were dealing with plant populations as high as fourteen thousand plants per acre to a low of three thousand plants per acre. Data were gathered examining such factors as the number of man-hours each spacing required from transplanting to stripping, the quality and yield of each spacing and the chemical composition. In addition, some of the work required measurements of individual stalk diameters and heights and weights from both green and cured tobacco. The need to take into account such factors as stalk size and quality was an integral part of this research. Tobacco grown close together tends to have a stalk that is smaller in diameter and tends to weigh less than tobacco grown on a wide spacing. This makes for less weight per stick during harvest; however, there are fewer sticks on the wider spacings. Quality also is affected by plant spacing; tobacco grown on a close spacing has a thin-bodied leaf that is lighter in both color and weight than leaves from tobacco grown on a wide spacing. In the days before filtered cigarettes, this was advantageous for the farmer who grew his tobacco on a close spacing. However, in 1989's market, where buyers wanted dark, heavy-bodied tobacco, tobacco grown on a wider spacing sold better. The data suggested that a spacing that has between 8,500 to 9,500 plants per acre would produce the best results. With plant populations such as this, the grower did not have to handle as many plants as in close spacings, nor would the plants have the large stalk diameter of plants grown on wide spacings. The grower would save on labor and still maintain high yields and good quality.

   * *Cost effectiveness of housing tobacco.* Mundy and Isaacs, along with Dr. Zacharias Henry of the University of Tennessee's Agricultural Engineering Department, led the way in these studies. Research focused on the areas of curing, labor and building costs. In 1980, a barn was constructed for the purpose of studying curing density in burley tobacco. This barn was designed so that two acres of tobacco could be housed in the amount of space usually required to house one acre of tobacco. To accomplish this, the barn was tiered three and a half feet wide instead of the traditional four and a half feet. Spacing between the sticks of tobacco on the tiers was reduced from the standard one foot to six inches. The sticks held six stalks of tobacco compared to the normal five. All of these factors added up to doubling the capacity of the barn. The problem with housing tobacco in such high density lies in the curing process. Tobacco that is hung this close restricts the flow of fresh air and is subject to house burn, molding and even rotting. The cured tobacco is usually black and of little use to tobacco buyers. To overcome this problem, Dr. Henry designed the barn with large fans in the top so that fresh air could be moved through the barn constantly. The movement of air, even if it were moisture laden, kept the tobacco from succumbing to the perils associated with closely hung

Left: A tall multitier curing barn near Springfield, Tennesee. *Photo by Chris Bickers.*

Below: A burley barn near Springfield, Tennessee. *Photo by Chris Bickers.*

As production of burley has concentrated on fewer farms, large new burley barns have cropped up. This one stands near Lafayette, Tennessee. *Photo by Chris Bickers.*

In the 1990s, farmers economized on the cost of building curing facilities by hanging sticks in wooden structures that could be covered with black plastic. *Photo by Chris Bickers.*

tobacco. The movement of air also speeded up the curing process. This meant, theoretically at least, that two crops could be put through the barn in the same season. In the case of this particular barn, a total of four acres could be cured in the same amount of space that one acre of tobacco would require in a conventional system. In order for this system to work, however, everything must fall into place throughout the entire growing season. Delays in transplanting or harvesting caused by the weather or other circumstances could ruin any chance of running two crops through the barn. To exemplify this, only once during the eight growing seasons in which these density tests were conducted were two crops cured in this barn in one season.

   * *Use of cable hoist technology.* The search for a means of reducing labor requirements in housing tobacco led to the development in Kentucky of a cable hoist system for hanging tobacco. In this system, the sticks of tobacco are stuck into a rail, which is two pieces of lumber bolted together with blocks of wood at either end to create a space for the tobacco sticks. The rail is attached to a steel cable and lifted up into the barn by mechanical means.

   The station first began studies dealing with the cable hoist system in the late 1970s. In a section of the new burley barn, several rails were linked together with small-diameter steel cable and lifted into the barn with a hand crank once the rails were filled with sticks of tobacco. The rails were left suspended on the cables until the tobacco was cured. A major problem with the system was the stress placed on the cables by the loaded rails. This stress resulted in broken cables on several occasions—a situation that was not only inconvenient but dangerous as well. So personnel from the university's Agricultural Engineering Department modified the cable hoist system. The rails were taken up into the barn with the use of a hydraulic hoist. Cables suspended from the top of the barn were run through the ends of the rails and attached to hydraulically controlled pulleys. One man using a handheld control box would then raise the loaded rails into the barn. Once the rail was in the proper position, it was placed on specially designed supports in the barn. This new system eliminated the stress factor of the old system and made the operation much safer. Labor studies by Mundy and Isaacs focused on the procedure of loading the sticks of tobacco onto the rails. Comparisons are made between loading the rails in the field and transporting them to the barn and bringing the tobacco to the barn and then loading it onto the rails. Times for both of these methods were then compared with the traditional method of hanging tobacco.

   This study was conducted throughout much of the 1980s, with data being collected not only on the amount of labor used but also on the effect that handling tobacco with this system had on the quality and yield. In the final analysis, it was judged that the hoist system did eliminate the need for costly labor used in hanging tobacco, but the amount of time required in the process of loading the rails offset this advantage to a certain degree.

The main difference in the two methods lies in where and in what type of labor was required. The grower could use less-experienced—and less-expensive—labor with the hoist system than he could with the conventional method of hanging tobacco due to the fact that not just anyone is capable of climbing into a barn and standing spread-eagle on two narrow tier poles while handling sticks of green tobacco that might weigh as much as forty pounds each. A negative factor in the hoist system is the high initial cost for installing the system. Construction of a facility or the renovation of an old barn would be necessary if the system were used. This cost, coupled with the expense of cable, lumber for the rails and the hoist itself, makes the system unfeasible for many growers. Because of these factors, the future of the cable hoist system seems to lie in the hands of those growers who produce a minimum of fifteen acres of tobacco per season.

Alternative housing. A project dealing with barn costs was undertaken at the station in 1989. In this study, researchers wanted to build a structure capable of housing tobacco for a minimum cost. The purpose of this study was to give people who were interested in expanding their tobacco operation but were reluctant to invest in the high cost of a conventional tobacco barn an alternative solution to the problem of housing their tobacco. The structures that resulted from this project were open-sided sheds that utilized cheap roofing materials such as plastic, fiberglass and cardboard coated with tar. Some of these structures were designed so that one man could hang the tobacco in them while standing on a wagon. Others required one man in the barn and one man handing the tobacco off the wagon. In designing the structures in this way, the researchers hoped to show a savings not only in construction but in labor as well. Although the sides of the barns were left uncovered during the 1989 season, the cured tobacco showed little sign of weather damage. However, if a farmer wanted to protect his tobacco from the elements, all he need do was cover the sides with inexpensive plastic. These barns were built for a fraction of what a traditional tobacco barn would cost, and even though some of the materials used would have to be replaced annually, the overall savings still favored them over the traditional barn. Timing studies comparing the amount of man-hours required to hang these new structures versus the conventional high-tiered barns also favored the new design.

Other efforts by the station of reducing costs and labor have been aimed at improving the way in which certain tasks involved in tobacco production are performed. The two tasks most often addressed in these efforts have been harvesting and market preparation.

Throughout the years, there have been a number of attempts to invent a machine capable of harvesting tobacco. Various individuals, as well as private companies and agricultural institutions, have been involved in these attempts. Although some of these inventions have been patented, they have never caught on with farmers. The reasons for this are several, with cost and practicality among them, but the primary reason for the failure of mechanical tobacco harvesters lies in the inherent nature of tobacco itself. To be properly harvested, tobacco must be handled with a certain degree of care to ensure against damage to the quality of the leaves or even the complete loss of the leaves. This degree of care has been difficult to attain.

Most of the work done at the station dealing with mechanical tobacco harvesters was conducted by Dr. Henry of the university's Agricultural Engineering Department. Henry developed several different prototypes of tobacco harvesters but ran into the same problems that have plagued others who pursued this same goal:

 * *Two handed stripping.* Researchers have had better luck in designing a system aimed at speeding up the stripping process. One, which was originally designed by a Washington County, Tennessee farmer named Park Range, utilizes a carousel-type wheel to hold the sticks of tobacco while workers strip off the leaves. Each wheel is designed to hold four sticks of tobacco and is made so that the height is adjustable to the workers' height. The main advantage of the carousel system is that it allows workers to use both hands for stripping the leaves from the stalk, whereas in the conventional relay system, one hand was used to hold the stalk.

In studies conducted at the experiment station by Mundy and Isaacs, three workers—one for each grade—were positioned around the carousel. One man loaded the sticks onto the wheel and pulled the lug grade; he then swung the wheel around to the next man, who pulled his grade and turned the wheel to the man pulling the tip grade, who, after pulling his grade, removed the stick from the wheel. This process went in continuous fashion with workers helping one another if one fell behind. The leaves were placed in bale boxes strategically positioned around the carousel, and specially designed containers were close by for the empty stalks and sticks. Timing studies have shown that by handling tobacco in a bulk manner such as this, the grower can reduce the time spent stripping tobacco by nearly one-third. To the bewilderment of researchers, however, the carousel has failed to gain much support from growers. This once again illustrates the

Some mechanical burley harvesters have been developed. This farmer near Tarboro, North Carolina—a new area for burley—has had good success using this Kirpy model harvester. *Photo by Chris Bickers.*

difficulty researchers at the station often face when trying to bring new ideas before the public.

* *Float bed plant production.* This method of growing transplants was brought to the attention of burley tobacco growers by Dr. Donald Fowlkes, the extension tobacco specialist at the University of Tennessee. In the system used at the time, seedlings were germinated in Florida and shipped in Styrofoam mini-flats. Once the plants arrived, they were transferred to larger Styrofoam trays filled with a special soil mix containing enough fertilizer to grow the plants to the size needed for transplanting in the field. Once the plants were in these large trays, they were placed in beds filled with water, where they floated until they were large enough to be transplanted in the field. There has been much evolution since in the process, and by the early twenty-first century, nearly all burley plants in the United States were produced in float beds, almost always in trays the farmer seeded himself in an on-farm greenhouse.

The work in the areas of tobacco breeding, costs and labor are vital aspects of the station's work. However, in today's uncertain tobacco market, the station has begun looking at other alternatives to tobacco as cash crops.

In 1982, the station started an apple orchard to study the feasibility of apples as a cash crop in east Tennessee. Other projects in this vein have included tomato variety tests and a project involving the double cropping of broccoli and tobacco within the same growing season. These projects, along with the ongoing research with cattle, forage crops and agronomic practices, are geared toward helping the farmer in today's ever-changing world.

The contributions made by the Tobacco Experiment Station to the American tobacco industry are immeasurable. The role played by the station in increasing American tobacco production has placed tobacco near the top of the list of U.S. agricultural exports. The economic benefits derived from this increased production have helped everyone involved in the U.S. tobacco industry. Of the groups that have benefited from the station's efforts, the farmers in the burley tobacco–producing states are among the highest recipients.

The work conducted at the station in the area of plant breeding is enough in itself to merit a debt of gratitude from the entire tobacco industry. From the early advances made against black root rot disease and the major breakthrough against wildfire with the development of Burley 21 on to today's varieties that combine multiple disease resistance with enormous yields and high quality, the station's tobacco-breeding program has had a tremendous impact on the tobacco industry.

In addition to its tobacco-breeding program, the work in other areas of tobacco production conducted at the station has been vital. Agronomic studies have resulted in breakthroughs in the areas of soil fertility; weed, insect and sucker control; plant populations; and time of harvest. The benefits derived by growers from the results of these studies are major. Although the station's main emphasis has been on tobacco, the contributions it has made in other areas of agriculture have also been important. Research in the areas of cattle production, small grains, forage crops, fruits and vegetables has helped in the promotion of these commodities and has also found solutions to problems that confronted producers of these commodities.

This divergence and the ability to be flexible enough to adapt to the ever-changing needs of the farmer have always been among the station's strong points. This flexibility, as well as innovativeness, can be seen today in the work dealing with labor needs and production costs that is currently being conducted at the station.

Finally, the Tobacco Experiment Station's main mission has been to serve the ordinary farmer. Throughout its nearly sixty years of existence (through 1989), this has been true, and it will continue to hold true for however long the station remains in existence.

A HISTORY OF TOBACCO AUCTIONS

The high point in the burley tobacco season during its glory years was the sale of the crop at an auction warehouse. It became more than a marketing transaction—for a few months every year, it was a way of life. "I really miss the warehouse business," says Jim Ed Cozart of Abingdon. "There was something kind of exciting about the opening day. You would see people leaving the auction, and you knew they would soon be out of debt."

Cozart remembers that when farmers came to warehouses, they would frequently stay the night. "We had sleeping quarters in the upper part of the building where the farmers could sleep there if they wanted to. And they could quarter their horses or mules in the basement."

Warehousing was a family business for Cozart. "My dad decided in 1922 that he would build a warehouse so farmers could deliver their tobacco in Abingdon, and he built it on Main Street and called it the Farmers Tobacco Warehouse," he says. "I remember it was a concrete block building. It burned down long ago, but many others were built, and Abingdon gained the reputation of being a market town for burley. Before long, we had two sets of buyers. That was an advantage for the farmer. It meant he got it sold quicker."

Jeff Aiken of Tedford, Tennessee, remembers, "We tied our tobacco in hands in those days and put it in baskets. Once we loaded those baskets on an old truck, we would haul them to the warehouse in Greeneville. We sold at Adams warehouse and the Growers warehouse and some others."

Now, since the contracting era began, he markets in Rogersville, Tennessee, with R.J. Reynolds. "It is quite a difference," he says. "I make an

Burley tied in hands and loaded on baskets awaits sale in an auction warehouse in Greeneville, Tennessee, in the early 1970s. *Photo by Bob Hurley.*

appointment, go through the line, the buyer ascertains the grade and I get paid. It is certainly not as colorful as the auctions in the old days."

The markets would open three days before Thanksgiving, he says. "That was considered the beginning of the marketing season. I remember one warehouse had a warm morning stove in its office. Farm people would gather there to visit."

The people who grew the burley were the center of attention at market time. "There was a lot of excitement when we got to the market," Aiken remembers. "There were bankers out giving calendars and ink pens. Farmers were welcome indeed in Greeneville in the fall. In the spring, we didn't get quite as good a reception."

And they didn't always get the reception they were hoping for from the buyers. Joe McNeil, a farmer from Vilas, North Carolina, remembers how one year a neighbor with about one-tenth of an acre of tobacco sold it at the Big Burley warehouse in Boone. "The price he got was quite a bit less than he was expecting. He was so sad, he was crying. He thought he must have been robbed. 'Why did they steal my tobacco?' he said. That caught my attention because it showed how little people had in those days. Tobacco was their only way of getting money."

HOW AUCTIONING GOT STARTED

The first industry on the American continent was started by John Rolfe of Jamestown (more widely famed as the husband of Pocahontas); at the same time, this was the first export industry in 1613, when he shipped two hundred pounds of native tobacco from his farm to England. This tobacco was of desirable flavor to the English, and as a result, they demanded more. Rolfe smuggled the seed from a sweeter and milder type of tobacco, grown in Varina, Spain, into the colonies and began to produce a more desirable product. As a result, demand from Europe rose even more. Thus, Rolfe named his plantation Varina Farms. It continues to be a working farm today, even though tobacco hasn't been planted on the land in almost three hundred years.

The commercial venture initiated by Rolfe reversed from failure to success the fate of the colonists trying to settle on American soil. It also gave the British government its first success in establishing a new colony on another

A burley-curing barn on a country road in Greene County, Tennessee. *Photo by Bob Hurley.*

continent. It had tried and failed four times previously. Tobacco trade from Jamestown had made the difference.

Upon returning from his first trip to England in 1616, Rolfe discovered the effect his venture had had on colonial planters. It was growing everywhere around Jamestown and as far west as the land known today as Richmond. Planters were beginning to neglect crops that were needed for food. This practice invited the first governmental intervention. In 1616, the deputy governor of Jamestown sought to bring balance in agriculture production by disallowing anyone to grow tobacco unless they also grew two acres of corn. This act provided, at least to some degree, better variation in agriculture production and encouraged the population to realize the importance of reaping broader sustenance from the new land. However, demand for tobacco in England skyrocketed, and the New World responded with increased production of this different form of "gold."

The door was opened for planters to use tobacco as a way to trade for goods manufactured in the mother country. Utensils, implements, foods, clothing, home supplies and other necessities could not be manufactured in the colonies. England was centuries ahead in industry, and it was a natural trade evolution for the colonists to begin bartering with exporters in trading tobacco for imported goods. At this point, there were basically three segments of society: the planter, the merchant and the political leaders (the latter two were, in many cases, one and the same). The political leaders were appointed by the king. Sometimes a planter could easily fit into all three social categories, but as the population increased, more planters found themselves at the bottom of the social and economic spectrum.

Currency was not available in the colonies, so it became necessary to use tobacco as a substitute. The process weaved its way from the planter to the merchant and then to exportation. Debts were paid in tobacco pounds. Then the planter would reenter into debt to the merchant for the cost of another crop, as well as additional goods, and remain in debt to him until another crop was presented to the latter for settlement.

The merchant, in turn, would receive the tobacco, export it to his customers in England, trade for goods, import the goods and again trade to the planter for more tobacco. Tobacco was usually delivered at the wharf (sometimes referred to as the rolling house, tobacco magazine or storage house), conveniently located at a suitable port along the river. It was packed tightly in barrels of sizable capacity, called hogsheads. Each end, or head, of the hogshead was built so a stout pole could be inserted through the hogshead to the other side, and it could be pulled into the shipping point by

A burley barn on a hill near Springfield, Tennessee, sheltering a scaffold wagon that could be used to cure burley also. *Photo by Chris Bickers.*

oxen or other means. When the merchant or receiver took it into possession, the planter was given a tobacco note, which was used to pay any and all debts. After a short period, the planter discovered that the merchant, as a rule, didn't examine the goods inside the hogshead. Instead, he placed it on board the ship and sent it to England along with other cargo.

This invited a practice among planters known today as "nesting." Nesting of tobacco is simply placing the good-quality tobacco in the top of the hogshead and bad quality at the bottom or deep inside to conceal it from the merchant. Thus, even if the merchant should question the integrity of the planter and look inside, he surely wouldn't tear it apart and waste a lot of time trying to qualify it. By 1619, the practice of nesting had risen to such proportions that English customers began to complain to colonial merchants and to the authorities of England. As a result, the second government intervention was imposed on tobacco producers of the New World. This was the first general inspection law passed by the House of Burgesses, mandating that all tobacco offered for exchange and found to be "mean" in quality by the magazine custodian be burned. In 1620 and 1623, this law was amended to provide for the appointment of sworn men in each settlement to condemn all bad tobacco. In 1630, an act was passed prohibiting the sale or acceptance of inferior tobacco in payments of debts. The commander of each plantation or settlement was authorized to appoint two or three competent men to help him inspect all tobacco offered in payments of debts. If the inspectors declared the tobacco mean, it was burned, and the delinquent planter was disbarred from planting tobacco. Only the General Assembly could remove this disability. From 1619 through 1785, there were numerous laws passed in Virginia designed to protect the purchaser from inadvertently buying or trading for nested tobacco. None of these laws effectively served its purpose. With each new law came new and more innovative methods by the planter to discretely insert bad tobacco along with the good. The merchant, being aware of this ever-increasing and damaging practice, and not having the collective defense against it, responded by dropping the value per pound. Sir Francis Wyatt sought to deal with nesting by reducing the yield per planter. In 1621, he required each planter to limit his tobacco production to one thousand plants, with no more than nine leaves each or a maximum net yield of one hundred pounds. The effort was designed to discourage the planter from bringing a larger and more bulky hogshead to port. The planter easily found ways to circumvent this, and Wyatt's order was soon rescinded.

In 1629, the maximum cultivation allowed each planter had risen to three thousand plants, plus an additional one thousand for non-laboring women and each child. By this time, the export figure had climbed to 1,500,000 pounds. In less than twenty years after the settlement of a new continent, a commodity had been established that would serve as the major commercial factor in a new society. It was the fuel of survival and promise. As with any social and economic phenomenon, the situation required some form of order, authority and organization.

The beginning of tobacco trade was the beginning of America. If colonization was to succeed, clearly there had to be a structure of trade that would promote social and economic progress, not just for the colonist, but also in the interest of the European investors who had an economic stake in the fate of the New World.

Colonial tobacco production was the major influence in geographic expansion along the rivers and bays of the Virginia peninsula and northward into what are now Delaware, Maryland and Pennsylvania. Production was demanding on coastal soil. There were no agronomic instructions at that time, no fertilizer effective enough to replenish the soil from one year to the next, so the planter was forced to relocate and clear new fields every two or three years in order to get a satisfactory return on his crop. Some moved north and some moved south, but most, along with their families and laborers, moved westward into inland areas. There were other factors that promoted expansion. The planter needed "elbow room" in addition to his desire to put distance between himself and authority. The abundance of navigable rivers up and down the eastern coast allowed flexibility in choosing new areas of production. Tobacco was saturating the eastern coastal areas, including North Carolina.

In a few short decades, tobacco was the consuming factor in colonial America. It dominated all social economic life in Virginia, which, of course, was the focus of the New World. It regulated the life of all commercial interest more than any product of a modern community. In 1633, it became the basic measure of value. That same year, it was demonetized by an act of the assembly, but the act was completely ignored by the people. In 1642, another act restored its monetary uses. Thereafter, debts not contracted in tobacco were not recoverable by law. The golden leaf was accepted as payment for taxes, purchases of wives and payments to preachers and the military (settlement guards). In 1660, the Lord Proprietors of Carolina organized a plan to develop colonies in what is now North Carolina. After King Charles II took the throne, he granted a vast area from Spanish Florida to the southern border of Virginia and from the Atlantic to the Pacific that was to become the Carolinas. One of the promises made to the king was that settlers of this area would not produce tobacco. This promise was made largely to appease the leadership in Virginia and Maryland who complained that opening up territory to the south would only add more trade competition and increase the already over-produced crop. However, settlers had already entrenched themselves in the Carolina area and had begun tobacco production before the colony was granted by Charles II. The Carolina settlers were putting more distance between themselves and authority, as well as finding new tobacco-producing soil. The increasing movement to the outskirts of settled territory, as well as the ingenuity of planters within settlements, gave constant rise to the ease of avoiding the regular barrage of laws dealing with nesting tobacco.

By 1644, the practice was so obvious that merchants and dealers began putting collective pressure on English rule to come to their aid in arresting the problem. Planters had begun to hide tobacco stalks, tree leaves and other worthless objects deep within hogsheads. Some planters even implanted liquor, starch and spikes into hogsheads. Any bill with which Parliament could come forth resulted only in taxing the imaginations of the planters. In 1666, Virginia leaders convinced producers in the Carolinas and Maryland that supply was beginning to exceed demand and it would be in the interest of the three colonies to abstain from production for one year. An agreement was made to this effect, only to be vetoed by Lord Baltimore. The veto served as an incentive to Carolina planters to open more cultivatable land and continue production below the Virginia border. In 1669, the Albemarle Assembly of North Carolina passed a law designed to attract more settlers into Carolina. This caused great concern to Virginians, who were already hostile to the Carolina settlers because of increased trade competition. Consequently, in April 1679, the Virginia General Assembly passed a law that prohibited tobacco from being shipped out of the Carolina colony, or "Rogues Harbor," as the colony had come to be called. This act by the assembly remained in place for almost one hundred years but had no real effect on tobacco trade coming out of the southern colony since the planters were as astute at smuggling into Virginia as they were in continuing to nest tobacco.

By 1731, the Privy Council in London realized the economics of commerce in the Carolinas and repealed the law of 1679. Even so, all tobacco produced, whether in Virginia or Carolina, was referred to as "Virginia" tobacco.

Between 1619, when the first law dealing with nesting tobacco was imposed, and 1730, numerous legislative efforts were brought forth to deal with this issue. All inspection laws passed between 1619 and 1641 were repealed, except the Act of 1630, which prohibited the sale or acceptance of inferior tobacco in payments of debts. The Act of 1630 remained in force until 1760. In 1723, the General Assembly passed an act authorizing the county courts to build warehouses at public expense. These were built for the sake of expediency within a mile of a public port, or landing, to ensure closer observation and policing of inspection laws. Governor Spotswood of Virginia introduced an act that would require licensed inspectors at warehouses. This was opposed by Colonel William Byrd and ultimately was vetoed by the Privy Council of London.

While the reason for opposition from Colonel Byrd is not clear, we can locally speculate on the Privy Council of London. Colonization of the New World was moving into a second century. The fruits of European investors and governments were being born from colonial fields of tobacco. Human and governmental greed had deeply ingrained itself through this trade—a trade that had its roots in North America but its reward in European commerce. The difficulty in regulation, by government enforcement, for the assurance of maximum profit for the mother country came through the distance between the governed and the governors. Even though the colonies were visited from time to time by English rule and there was appointed authority in the colonies, it was impossible for the Crown to maintain an objective view of the day-to-day business process on American soil. While nested tobacco continued to pour into Europe along with complaints, some justified and some not, from tobacco merchants, the Crown, because of the distance and lack of perception of the nature of the local scene, was unable to comprehend a true formula for correction. That, to a large extent, was left to local authorities, who, even at close range, were at a loss to deal with this persistent problem.

In 1730, after 110 years of legislative failure, the Virginia General Assembly passed the most comprehensive inspection bill ever introduced. In part, the act provided that no tobacco was to be shipped to England, except in hogsheads, cases or casks, without having been inspected at one of the legally established warehouses; thus, the shipment of bulk tobacco was prohibited. Two inspectors were employed at each warehouse, and a third was summoned in case of a dispute between the two regular inspectors. These officials were bounded and were forbidden under heavy penalty to pass bad tobacco, engage in tobacco trade or take rewards. Tobacco offered in payments of debts, public or private, had to be inspected under the same conditions as that to be exported. The inspectors were required to open the hogsheads and extract and carefully examine two samples. All trash and unsound tobacco was to be burned in the warehouse kiln in the presence of the owner and with his consent. If the owner refused consent, then the entire hogshead would be destroyed. After it was sorted, the good tobacco was repacked, and the planter's distinguishing mark, net weight and tare weight, as well as the name of the inspector and the warehouse, were stamped on the hogshead. The Act of 1730 was a desperate governmental effort to lay to rest, once and forever, the bad habit of planters.

As time passed, Europeans, who for many reasons were dissatisfied with their plight in the mother country and who had heard about the promise of riches from tobacco production in the New World, began to immigrate to the Tidewaters of Virginia, Maryland and the Carolinas. By the turn of the eighteenth century, tobacco exports from Carolina had risen to 800,000 pounds annually. Virginia and Maryland combined were exporting over 22 million pounds to Europe. The intensity of the nesting problem paralleled the rising population, as well as the volume of tobacco production. There was another purpose besides quality control integrated into the Act of 1730: to bring about some degree of order in the marketing system. The Carolina colony, which was rapidly becoming a major tobacco exporter, using suitable waters around Port Roanoke (Edenton) to ship tobacco to Scotland, adopted a similar inspection act in 1754.

Even with this comprehensive bill, problems continued. While marketing was beginning to take some form of order and organization, disputes over quality and prices were regularly initiated by either seller or buyer. The buyer used price reduction as a weapon against the prospects of receiving undesirable tobacco. The planter would cry foul. The government inspector would intervene and attempt to settle the matter. As nature has it, inspectors often yielded to the side that was more willing to discreetly pass along financial rewards to supplement the meager government pay. This practice, like that of nesting, pretty soon became general knowledge among all who frequented inspection stations. As the late eighteenth century approached, the Act of 1730, just as all efforts before it, became a helpless tool in tobacco inspection. Inspectors lost credibility, both with the merchant, even though he traditionally had better "persuasion" resources, and with the planter. Both often demanded re-inspection by someone whom they held in higher esteem and appeared to be more competent in the judgment of quality leaf. Distrust increased among participants of tobacco trade and led to the decrease in the value of the tobacco note. There were some cases in the mid-eighteenth century, especially if the buyer and seller knew each other as men of integrity and honesty, where purchases would be made on the plantation and debt would be settled on the spot. In the event of a dispute under these circumstances, two reputable and competent neighbors were called in to solve the matter. This nature of tobacco trade—private agreement, placing less importance on government inspectors while at the same time allowing planters and merchants to keep a close eye on inspection stations—continued well into the later part of the eighteenth century.

By 1775, the Inspection Act of 1730 had been rendered useless in ensuring honest trading at the official inspection station. It was repealed. For the next year, purchases at the plantation increased, and the merchant himself was the inspector. Or the merchant would visit the warehouse during the official inspection, seek out the owner of the better-quality tobacco without using the judgment of the inspector and make a private offer. This method became popular, and shortly planters were preparing their crops to be transported to the warehouses frequented by the greatest number of merchants. Prices under this new twist seemed higher than for those in the inspection process. Independent market houses, open street markets and warehouses began to appear in small towns and settlements throughout the Tidewater areas and, by 1810, as far west as Lynchburg, Virginia. At this point, four ingredients of the present-day tobacco auction system were in place: warehouses, which were established by the Act of 1712; the Act of 1730, which resulted from the need to ensure fairness in trade; the displaying of tobacco to attract merchants; and the beginning of small market towns and commercial demand. This process had played a major role in the continued rise in shaping the structure and economic growth of colonial America. No one can argue that tobacco had been the driving force in social, political and economic progress in the New World. This commerce had greatly influenced European attitude toward the colonies. The demand in England for American tobacco products, tax revenue gains and the assurance given European investors who cast their lot on the New World all stemmed from the golden weed. It gave the North American settlement the status of favorite son to the British.

Establishing and maintaining a credible and orderly system of production control and organized marketing and, to the best degree possible, ensuring the delivery of quality tobacco, first to the marketplace and then to England, was smart business as far as the government was concerned. The colony had a different stake in the tobacco business. It had struggled for over a century to take root and grow. Tobacco was the one commodity behind whatever success enjoyed thus far. Society was, for all practical purposes, ruled by it. Those who were favored by the king had been given enormous tracts of land on which to start new lives. They led the way in tobacco production. The less blessed followed their lead. Some of the latter carved out economic and social growth, and some didn't. Nevertheless, colonial society was completely and hopelessly dependent on tobacco, and all knew that individual and collective success was governed by the fate of a year's crop. Universities were being erected by tobacco money, factories were beginning to appear as the result of tobacco trade, new settlements were constantly being opened and woodlands were being cleared in every direction to allow more room for crops. Villages and towns were popping up, and local, regional and colonial governments were occupied daily with tobacco issues. The people were vulnerable to the direction of trade. Tobacco problems meant social and economic problems, and to leave them unsolved meant social economic upheaval. Maximum social yield from this crop could only be ensured by the ease with which the process weaved its way from seed to consumer. A multiplicity of factors influenced that process, all of which surfaced at some point or another along the journey. The human characteristic of the colonist to prevail in commerce—especially since, at this time, the burden lay on one commerce alone—came into play as the planter prepared his tobacco for presentation at the first stop past the curing huts. He continually gambled that the merchant wouldn't discover his practice and expose him for trying to pass bad wares. The merchants lost at the game for a short while but, being the more influential of the two groups, finally prevailed and brought governmental authority down on the planter. This only challenged the ingenuity of the planter in staying a step ahead of the merchant. The merchant responded by advocating more comprehensive laws relating to inspection. For almost two hundred years, this game was played by these factors in tobacco trade. Nothing worked to satisfaction.

In 1776, the colonial leadership declared independence from English rule. Tobacco, which had traditionally been the sovereign glue for the colonist, again proved its value. It was used as collateral to obtain loans by which the first Continental Congress was formed and Revolutionary battles were fought and won. The success of the American Revolution, financed by tobacco, brought us freedom and an autonomous government: the United States of America. Yet, in all the gusto of a new nation and all the promise of growth and prosperity, our young and vibrant country had not successfully dealt with the age-old problem of fairness and order in its chief commerce.

Tobacco marketing, now under domestic rule, had gone through several phases since early Jamestown, but problems still existed at the point of sale. Even with continued marketing problems, tobacco commerce had effectively been the driving force behind expansion from the Tidewater area well inland to Richmond and Petersburg and as far west as Lynchburg. The nature of the problems had influenced the appearance of markets in these and other towns on the western perimeter of civilization. As government inspection warehouses declined in the Tidewater area after the beginning of the nineteenth century, so did tobacco production. The adventurous population, who wanted to continue producing and marketing its crops, moved westward. There was a decline in the number of inspection stations, not just in the Tidewater area but also in general. Just before 1800, there were seventy-two official inspection stations in Virginia, thirteen of which had been shut down by 1810. Fifty-four were concentrated around Richmond. In 1816, 90 percent of tobacco brought to market was inspected at the Richmond, Petersburg or Lynchburg stations. This meant that while commerce was moving out of its original geographical area, it was beginning to concentrate in fewer towns. Until this phase in social growth, tobacco had ensured the survival and prosperity of the colonist. It had been the conduit that, with daily activity around the rolling house, inspection stations, bartering areas and commercial trading in the villages, had brought the local communities together and had formed their social attitudes, habits and outlook as inhabitants of a new world.

Over a span of two hundred years, we have seen how tobacco trade dominated the development of a new nation. We have also seen how the marketing phase of that trade influenced society and government. While the issue of ensuring quality was the focus of laws, rules and regulations, as well as public reactions to the shortcomings of both planter habits and government authority, the resulting gain contributed to building a secure and progressive base in which colonists developed the American society.

After the War of 1812, speculation in tobacco trade began growing at an increasing rate. Speculation in tobacco trade (as in other trades) means buying at a low price and selling at a higher price, and doing so as soon as possible so as to not require the overhead of any significant amount of facilities, inventories or other profit-eating costs. Inspectors, while legally forbidden to engage in this or any other practice that would hinder their objectivity or fairness, had very discretely been involved in speculating in tobacco trade for some time without having their hands called by the public or government. For two centuries, they had either been too discrete to be caught red handed or were making it worthwhile for those affected. Both planters and buyers claimed to have suffered at the hand of the inspector. This, along with the natural change in marketing attitudes of sellers, gave birth to the adoption, in some market towns, of a tried and attractive new twist in sales used by French marketing for ages: the auction. Some planters would bring their crops to the market center, decide for themselves what might be an appealing price for their crops and either cry and bid or employ someone else, perhaps the inspector, to do the job for them. The intention was to establish competition among purchasers. This novel new concept was not practiced in all markets at first, but within a few years, it began to spread into a wider area. However, no problems were solved with the auction. By law, inspectors could not engage in crying the bid for anyone with whom they had financial connections, unless (as the law stated) they were asked by that person. This legal loophole protected this traditional, but illicit, practice.

By the middle of the second decade of the nineteenth century, private auctioneers begin advertising themselves for hire at warehouses. The first of these was a gentleman from Richmond named H.B. Montague, who responded to the festering problem. In November 1827, he advertised himself in the *Richmond Inquirer* as an "Independent Tobacco Auctioneer, one of integrity." While others before him had, in fact, begun this practice, without regarding it as auctioneering, Montague set the stage for the auctioneering commerce. This meant that one who considered himself a private auctioneer could hire out to the planter, enter the market and represent that planter without government ties.

Soon, the importance of the inspector diminished. The seller took his tobacco to the market that attracted the largest number of buyers and had the most competitive atmosphere and hired an auctioneer to cry the bid for his crop. The inspector was not involved in the process under this new system, since the buyers had begun their own inspecting before making a bid. Using all the loopholes, the inspector then saw an opportunity to offer himself, in addition to his government responsibilities, as a "crier." He also offered himself as a commission merchant. Virginia law continued its attempts to deal with the illicit practice of the inspectors doubling as auctioneers, but to no avail. In 1849, the General Assembly revised its laws governing the perimeters of inspectors to such an extent that they had broader leverage and could operate either as inspectors or auctioneers, whichever brought them the highest revenue at the moment.

The role of tobacco between 1612 and the second decade of the nineteenth century was exemplified in several areas. First, as discussed, tobacco was the lifeblood in establishing a successful settlement in the New World. There was a great deal at stake, both with the English underwriters and with the settlers who were seeking a new way of life. Once the commerce was established, natural trade evolution took its course, and mutual dependency between the mother country and its colony became well entrenched. To England, it was a new source of wealth and world power. To the colonist, it was a ray of light on the horizon of freedom from whatever suppression had been imposed by former European governance. In spite of the uncertainties, there was hope. That hope was a commodity that the Old World was demanding more and more. There had to be some degree of organized route from the planter to the consumer across the sea. That route included the point of marketing, and marketing caused one of the biggest problems. In responding to this problem, government-imposed rules and regulations, while not effectively solving the problem, served as an important factor in encouraging the settlers to expand. Another factor in expansion, of course, was the need to find fresh soil on which to plant crops, but equally as important was the desire of the planter to put as much distance between himself and nosy government as was practically possible without being out of range of financial support. As expansion occurred, marketplaces followed, and as marketplaces appeared, population density increased. The domino effect proved to be a great force in the continued opening of new territory. Transportation on rivers, canals and roads frequented by tobacco hogsheads made expansion easier and more expedient. As new settlements sprang up and markets multiplied, inspectors became more numerous. These public figures, as we have pointed out, were appointed by the colonial leadership. The appointment, no doubt, was the ticket to influence among the planters and merchants. After all, who else could have such an impact on the life of a tobacco planter or tobacco merchant in a society that depended solely on the price of tobacco?

In human terms, this government official, whose judgment could make or break a planter in a moment's time or who could rob the merchant of his profits simply by the very attitude in which he surveyed the contents of a hogshead, was in an enviable position—one that allowed him a disproportionate share of public weight.

Even though the auction method of tobacco sales had not completely dominated marketing by the third decade of the nineteenth century, it had taken a strong foothold and was now being considered by both seller and buyer as preferable to the older process of meeting in the town square, presenting the goods and having the government inspector judge the quality and finally close the sale. The auction method contained several attractive elements that helped it gain popularity among all parties of trade. Even before the rhythmic chant of the auctioneer, the inspector, who by this time had taken on the role of "crier," created excitement in his attempt to stir up competition among buyers. He simulated a form of entertainment to the gathering street crowds and offered a bit of curiosity to a budding new village or town that otherwise sorely lacked amusement facilities. This early stage of auctioneering enhanced competition among buyers, who heretofore had used private bartering or "barn-door" buying at the plantation and other private means of purchasing. The approach from the buyer had been to negotiate in private so as not to give a competitive buyer the opportunity to lure the planter with a higher price.

The business was more in a public vein now than before. The auction offered buyers easier and more consolidated ways to make purchases. They didn't have the expense and time-consuming trouble of traveling into widely spaced towns and villages to fill their needs. The convenience of relative compactness for the buyer and the encouraged competition for the planter accelerated the process from the inspection stations, scattered great distances apart, to auctions. The added feature of free entertainment in the street kindled the fires of change from the old way to the new. It is safe to say that the old method of government inspection and trade, as well as the new method of private merchant inspection and auction, the increase in demand for tobacco and the ensuing demand for additional marketplaces or towns, played a major role in establishing many of today's major towns and metropolitan areas along the eastern seaboard.

Even though the inspection system remained intact long after the auction method emerged, it began to be more and more sectionalized. The novelty of the auction spurred new market towns and brought new promise to areas that had been slow in growth. In 1838, the method of curing bright tobacco, now referred to as flue-cured, was accidentally discovered just below the Virginia border in Caswell County, North Carolina. Flue-cured tobacco, unlike that which had been historically dark in color, was bright yellow and immediately brought more at sale than did the darker. This discovery on the Slade farm probably caused as much excitement about tobacco commerce as any single incident since John Rolfe found demand for the commodity in Europe. Of course, tobacco had proven its importance by this time, but with the population increase, the simultaneous increase in tobacco consumption and the discovery of a new kind of tobacco, the "bright" tobacco production made a sharp turn upward. The need for expediency on the sale became a critical factor.

Heretofore, sales were relatively uneventful in terms of marked excitement: the planter brought his crop to the marketplace and the merchant looked it over or, where government inspectors were still available, it was inspected. The inspector sometimes doubled as a crier and took bids on behalf of the planter. Offers were made and accepted or refused, and the transaction was completed. Now, the trend was moving to faster sales. Also, with the gradual diminishing of public inspections, merchants were more cautious in protecting themselves against bad tobacco. Private warehouses, which were now in the majority over government houses, were responding by holding loose-leaf sales. The loose-leaf sale, of course, meant that instead of bringing tobacco to market in hogsheads or casks, the planter had to present it in loose or un-prized (unpacked) form. It was easier to inspect in its entirety this way. Loose-leaf sales followed close behind the auction method, and in 1858, the first full-time loose-leaf tobacco warehouse was opened in Danville, Virginia, by Mr. Thomas Neal and associates. This set the stage for the contemporary tobacco sales and became known as the Danville System.

The Danville System, while setting a precedent, didn't eliminate the old method. That remained for decades to come. Tobacco production had moved westward into Kentucky, midwestern states and as far away as across the Mississippi River and had been broken down into types. The different types depended on location of production, kinds of soil in which they were produced or method of curing—artificial heat, air cured, sun cured or fire cured. Selling under the old method or new was determined by all these factors, plus the mandate from state government and wishes of those affected by a local scale. However, flue-cured tobacco, which will be our focus from this point, has been sold by the loose-leaf auction system since opening day of Neal's warehouse in Danville.

The concept of the loose-leaf auction system, which some historians suggest was the brainchild of a Dr. J.B. Stovall of Halifax County, Virginia, not only served the cause of expediency but also, more effectively, served to correct or at least arrest many discrepancies within the system of marketing. As we have stated, the practice of auctioning had been used for some time already. In Danville, it had been experimented with since 1837, but it wasn't used exclusively. Neal and his associates had to travel through tobacco-production areas and convince farmers to try the new auction system. He claimed, quite correctly, that his new way of marketing would eliminate many of the aggravations found in the old way: immediate pay to the farmer after the sale instead of the old way of having to wait for pay, a reduction of tobacco loss suffered before as the buyers and their associates would pull samples from lots when doing their own private inspections, a keener air of competition, the laborious job of prizing tobacco and having it shipped to Richmond and no fee to be paid for inspection. However, in 1960, Neal obtained authorization from the Virginia General Assembly to inspect tobacco and impose a fee on the farmer. For the buyer, the advantage lay in the fact that tobacco was in loose-leaf form and the risk of nesting was less than in prized tobacco. Neal and his associates also pointed out that the buyer had a better grade of tobacco to choose from since his method of sales would entice farmers to bring all their crops, including the best available, to Danville instead of to Richmond, Petersburg or Lynchburg.

On June 6, 1872, there was a new regulation passed, designed to help the federal government collect taxes from all tobacco dealers. This regulation stated that every farmer had to furnish to the government with a correct statement of all sales of leaf. Furthermore, the statement had to be furnished under oath. This regulation added yet another incentive for farmers to sell at an organized auction. Neal's warehouse responded by issuing a public statement saying that any farmer who sold at his warehouse, in addition to getting his pay immediately, would also receive a documented sales slip showing how much tobacco he had sold; thus, he would be in a position to answer any questions put to him by the government. This gave farmers even more incentive to sell at auction instead of directly to manufacturers.

Another incentive, more pertinent to Neal, was his desire to establish a local market in Danville that would arrest the practice of farmers traveling through to sell in Lynchburg. The completion of the Danville–Richmond railroad was the final accomplishment that gave Danville what it needed to attract added attention to growers and persuade them that their crops could be sold for the highest dollar on the Danville market. The railroad speeded the transportation route from market to manufacturer in Richmond. Other advantages offered by the loose-leaf auction were the convenience of selling tobacco under protective shelter instead of the earlier practice of bringing the crop to town and, with the assistance of a "town crier," announcing the arrival of tobacco by a blast of a bugle and then selling it from a farm wagon that stood in the street and finally carrying it to the factory to be weighed on old-fashioned sword balances or "steal yards and pea." Seller and buyer both liked the idea of a more organized and expedient selling method. The farmer also liked the prospects of receiving a more accurate weight by an impartial weigh master, and the buyer liked the change to more closely inspected quality of goods.

The stage had been prepared with most of the elements of our present-day auction system. However, the outbreak of the Civil War almost brought public trading of tobacco to a screeching halt, but not completely. While the disruption of the new method was greatly affected by the war between the North and South, the postwar period brought on a greater demand for tobacco grown principally by Confederate states. The Northern armies had penetrated into the southland and pilfered through storage houses, barns and pack houses, and they developed a taste for the bright flue-cured tobacco. No sooner had the war ended than they began sending orders southward for more. Washington Duke, who owned a small farm at Durham Station, North Carolina, returned home from his imprisonment by a Yankee soldier in a tobacco warehouse in Richmond to find most of the crop (produced by his family in his absence) stolen by Northern soldiers. Soon, he began receiving mail from up North asking for more bright tobacco. He responded by building a tobacco factory, which was nothing more than a small building his family used to beat cured tobacco leaves into tiny particles, bagging them and establishing a mail-order business into the North. At the same time, he began traveling around the region and hawking his trade. Within ten years, he was a millionaire.

With rise in demand came rise in production and marketing and the ever-increasing rise in the importance of tobacco at every rural crossroad in the South. All throughout the process of tobacco trade, transportation was limited, for the most part, by wagon roads and canals. The James, Rappahannock, Roanoke and Potomac Rivers were prominent arteries in transporting tobacco hogsheads from the inlands to market towns and ports. Roads had been carved out—some by planters, some by communities and some by counties and states—but tobacco progress demanded better and faster ways to get the crop to market. With demand increasing and warehouse numbers rising in both Virginia and North Carolina, warehousemen, who by their wealth accumulated through the market system were the most influential in local and state politics, realized the vested interest they had in promoting better transportation for farmers. They began bringing pressure on representatives in state and federal legislatures to have railroads built convenient to their places of business. These railroads would not only open up small towns and give them access to the larger industrial centers such as Richmond, but they would also provide better and faster transportation to tobacco manufacturing centers. Other types of commerce would benefit from the modernization of transportation as well. Thus, railroads systems, built to expedite transportation of tobacco from outlying areas into manufacturing facilities, served to bring a society that, even in the mid-nineteenth century, was scarcely populated closer together in commercial trade.

Along with the intensity of tobacco trade came support trade. As transportation was made faster and easier, trades of all goods supplying the tobacco industry and the gathering of civic and business interest began to increase. Tobacco towns grew at a rapid pace. Educational, religious, civic and business interests took root, and in many areas where there once was only a crossroad, such as Durham Station, thriving communities were established. Today, there are many examples of the influence tobacco marketing had on the success or failure of an area struggling to become an important locale for trade. Milton, North Carolina, just across the Virginia line, is one example. Its roots were fertilized by a tobacco market in the nineteenth century.

Tobacco warehouses, while built primarily for the purpose of organizing and selling large volumes of tobacco, served also as gathering places for other town functions. In most cases, they were the only facilities available to hold large crowds. Thus, they were used for various kinds of public events, such as political gatherings, religious services, rallies and official public meetings. After the loose-leaf auction became dominant, warehouses—unlike the old tobacco exchange, where only samples were brought inside for inspection while the remainder of the crop stayed outside—were built on a much larger scale with huge doors, windows and skylights and covered driveways for loading and unloading. They also had overnight accommodations that attracted farmers who lived more than a comfortable day's distance from the marketplace. Initially, most were built of wood; later, in the eighteenth century, brick was used for construction. Warehouses often covered acres of land. The owners then used the enormous size as an advertising factor.

David Y. Cooper of Henderson was one of the more knowledgeable tobacconists in the area, and his prowess in cutting the cost of building a new brick house in the early 1880s is illustrated when he invited his friends and customers to contribute a brick to its construction. Cooper's enthusiasm was such that most brought carts and wagonloads full of brick. Consequently, materials for outside construction were mostly free, and capital investment was at a minimum. Allen and Ginter, the leading cigarette manufacturer in Richmond at that time, brought a marble slab with silt tobacco leaves and an appropriate inscription.

Warehouse facilities were used for military musters before and during the Civil War. During World War II, they were used for rallies that encouraged citizens to buy Liberty Bonds and assist in fighting the war. In 1919, a new and short-lived tobacco warehouse was built in Statesville, North Carolina. Upon completion, the townsfolk held what was termed by contemporary observers the greatest fiddlers' convention in the history of Statesville. Even if it wasn't the greatest fiddling convention, it was certainly a great display of local pride. When Federal troops entered Richmond in 1865, warehouses were utilized for storage of various items valued by the U.S. government; these items included Confederate soldiers who had been taken prisoners (one of whom, as I have noted, was Washington Duke, who was routed to New Bern, North Carolina, before being released to walk home to Durham Station). Even today, tobacco warehouses in smaller towns are used for community gatherings of any significant size, including agriculture trade shows, school dances and such. With the end of the Civil War came the rebuilding of the South. Cotton had been a significant crop, but there wasn't another commodity that could compete with the economics of tobacco, especially with the additional increase in demand from Northern states. Reconstruction had begun in the South.

Tobacco, just as it had helped established colonies in 1612, rose to the cause of putting the South back on its feet. The new form of auction, started just before the war, which had brought easier, more organized, more convenient and competitive methods of selling tobacco, acted as a major lubricant in revenue exchange in the South as well as with Northern trade. Within six months after Lee surrendered to Grant at Appomattox, warehouses renewed their trade in Danville, and immediately tobacco manufacturing began in that town. Auction houses appeared, one behind the other, as the promise of financial stability was more apparent to those who engaged in the tobacco business. In 1869, the first tobacco association was formed in Danville, consisting of buyers, warehousemen and manufacturers. The Danville Tobacco Association, as it was called, was chartered for the purpose of "protecting the rights of all." In 1869, there were 10 buyers on the market. Within the next ten years, there were 125 buyers. Warehouse numbers increased from three to nine.

Farmers eagerly headed to Danville to sell their tobacco under the auction method, where they were assured keener competition than if they sold at private treaty or under the inspection system that still prevailed in Richmond, Lynchburg and other older markets. Another incentive to sell at auction was that unlike prized tobacco, the law did not required inspection for loose-leaf sales; it only required that tobacco be weighed honestly. This new method of selling tobacco caught on like wildfire, and while Danville took the lead, other villages fell in line. Durham opened its first market in 1870. Reidsville, Winston and Henderson followed closely behind. The stake Durham had in opening its market was the emergence of cigarette and smoking tobacco. W.T. Blackwell, who introduced Bull Durham smoking tobacco, hired Henry Reams to manage a small two-story building, converted into a warehouse, which held its first sale on May 18, 1871. The significance of this new house is that it marked the beginning of tobacco trade movement from Virginia into North Carolina. On opening day at Blackwell's warehouse, fifteen buyers showed up and purchased over fifty thousand pounds of bright tobacco.

Blackwell bought the first pile and most of the rest, which occupied both floors of the warehouse and part of the street outside the building. One historic aspect of this sale was that Mr. Dennis Talley of Dutchville Township in Granville County sold a load of extra bright yellow tobacco, known as "Dutchville wrappers," for $1.50 per pound. No doubt, Blackwell used this high price to incite more farmers to bring their tobacco to Durham instead of taking it to faraway Richmond or even Danville. In 1871, Durham sold about 700,000 pounds of tobacco, and in 1972, the poundage sold in Durham rose to over 2,000,000. The success of Blackwell's warehouse prompted others in Durham to enter the marketing business. Captain Edward J. Parrish, a Methodist preacher and barroom keeper who had been the auctioneer for Blackwell, opened his house in 1873. He also sidelined his marketing trade with a tobacco leaf dealership. Parrish solicited northern buyers for whom he wished to act as buying agent. By 1887, his house was selling 8,330,000 pounds per season. His auctioneering talents served as added entertainment to townsfolk and farmers alike. Parrish was one of the most successful tobacco warehousemen of his time. In 1888, he built a new and larger house and advertised it as the "Best Warehouse, Best Light, and Best Accommodations, for man and beast in N.C. or Virginia. Stable holds 200 horses."

In 1887, North Carolina, as part of an effort to shift the focus of attention away from Virginia, formed its first association: the North Carolina Tobacco Association. Captain Parrish was instrumental in this and served on the committee to make sure the state and its tobacco growers (and no doubt, the warehouse) received the recognition they deserved in producing a finer quality of tobacco. Part of the problem faced by producers in the Tarheel state was that northern buyers had always assumed that any tobacco bought from Virginia or North Carolina or advertised in northern papers was "Virginia" tobacco.

The *Daily Tobacco Plant* captured the scene of the market opening at Parrish's house as it described preparations: "The cloud of white canvas, or covers on Nissan wagons, poured into Durham from eight surrounding counties for the opening sale. Tobacco was placed on the new floor by Saturday in anticipation of the opening sale on Monday." J.J. Adcock, a prominent farmer from Granville County, led a cavalcade of farmers into the village amid shouts and a Methodist hymn. After the cavalcade, Parrish was presented a stylish fifty-dollar suit. Danville warehousemen responded with intensified efforts to lure farmers back into their fold, but for decades, North Carolina continued to enjoy an increased share of production and market. In 1908, Virginia boasted ten market towns, and North Carolina had forty-five. In 1919, North Carolina had sixty-four and Virginia twenty-three.

Where production was concentrated, markets formed, and warehouse numbers increased almost on an annual basis. By 1929, 83 percent of tobacco produced was sold in one-third of the market towns. Approximately 35 percent of the crop was sold at four markets: Danville, Rocky Mo[u]nt, Greenville and Wilson, with Danville being the only market outside North Carolina with a decent share of sales. The Danville System, as the auction method continued to be called, had not changed in concept since its beginning in 1858. Even markets with smaller volumes supported numerous warehouses. Oxford, Clarksville, South Boston, Creedmoor, Youngsville and many other towns became more and more dependent on tobacco money. Almost all businesses founded in the smaller markets, as well as in the larger ones, realized success or failure by the price farmers received for their crops. The price, in practically all cases, depended on demand for certain types and qualities within that type.

If a farmer brought good, ripe tobacco, cured just right and handled carefully, he could expect higher prices. If not, he would be disappointed.

But equally so, the farmer had to know the system and know the nature of the buyers. He had to school himself in producing a good crop. And warehousemen often went to great expense distributing publications to farmers on the art of planting, cultivation, harvesting, curing and, of course, marketing. It was in the best interest of the warehouseman to always have the best tobacco on his floor, as it would better attract the attention of buyers and ultimately bring a higher price for that warehouse. This, of course, could be used in advertising the house as getting higher averages for its customers. Even though the warehouseman served as the agent for the farmer, it was incumbent on the farmer to privately approach buyers, point out the location of his crop on the floor and promote an extra penny or two.

Tobacco warehouses were usually formed by more than one person. With the production perimeter widening constantly, it was expedient for ownership to be split among individuals who lived in strategic locations within traveling distance. These owners spent much of their off-season time drumming tobacco. "Drumming" is the art of soliciting farmers to sell at the warehouse owned by the drummer himself or at the house that had hired him to pay regular visits to the farmer and constantly remind him that the highest prices were to be had at the represented house. Many ploys were used in drumming tobacco, some ethical, some not and some bordering on being illegal. The Market Associations, which were formed in all markets eventually, were, by character, designed to eliminate or at least police these tactics. This element of the auction system, however, wasn't the most effective one. Farmers began to resist these drummers, partly because they were sometimes seen as a nuisance and partly because they made promises of higher prices than the warehouse could deliver. Suits were filed in many cases, and boards of trade, as the associates came to be known, were called on to put an end to the drummer. In 1904, Pitt County farmers launched an effort to establish a "cooperative" marketing situation, mainly to get rid of the drummer.

Winston-Salem, through the tobacco board of trade there, set up stringent regulations against the practice. Additionally, methods of solicitation were used to get market trade: offers of free transportation to the market, rebates, fees and commissions to farmers who brought their neighbors in to sell, promises to give extra enticement to buyers for a higher price on certain crops of tobacco and advances of loans to farmers, especially those who had borrowed their limit from banks. "First" sale was particularly attractive to farmers. A first sale meant that tobacco would be sold early in the day and the farmer didn't have to hang around for the better part of the day waiting for his tobacco to be sold. He could bring his load in the night before or early on the same day, sell it early and be home by dinner (noon). Some houses would hang out the FIRST SALE sign regardless of when the sale would start. This lured in the farmer under false pretenses, but after the crop was unloaded and placed on the floor, it was too late and too much trouble to wade through all the long rows and reload it to be taken to another house.

Sometimes farmers would relinquish their crops to a pin-hooker who just happened to be close by and observe the situation. A pin-hooker is a speculator: one who buys low and sells high. All in all, many stumbling blocks stood in the way of farmers who brought their year's investment to market, yet if the warehouseman was conscientious, he understood his dependency on continued patronage from the producer and would always act in the true sense of an agent. The stability of his business depended on this. The importance of the auction market to any town lay in its economic and social contributions. Before regulations required that tobacco not be transported more than one hundred miles from any county seat, farmers were at liberty to choose any warehouse they wished. This meant that no constraints were imposed on distance. The Oxford tobacco market, for instance, could solicit farmers from any area that grew tobacco. After South Carolina, Georgia and Florida began production, the perimeter widened drastically. Usually at least some percentage of the money passed at the market was spent locally. Warehouse checks, for the most part, were cashed in the town of sale. This increased "out of town" and new money flow in the community. Also, warehouse fees, which were established at 2.5 percent of sale, stayed in local hands.

Banks, which in many instances were formed in villages on the promise of tobacco markets, counted on tobacco money to keep the doors open and operating capital high. Not only banks but also every firm in the market area had a stake in how well the market did in volume and price. Opening day of tobacco markets brought out the best in town merchants. Street dances were staged, along with festive parades and special sales. Big banners proclaiming "Welcome Farmers" were hoisted high. Everyone was the farmer's friend when markets opened. Retailers would follow the farmers around and act as if they hadn't seen their best friends in years and the absence was unbearable. Con artists were plentiful. Merchants, who operated out of the backs of their buggies or, in later days, trunks of their cars hawking miracle goods, snake oils and such, were always a part of the festivities of opening day at the sale. There was a good reason for courting the farmer. He had brought his "gold" to the town to be transformed into cash—plenty of cash—and every enterprise wanted its fair share. The auction warehouse was the place of exchange, and those who wanted their share had to be on hand.

From the beginning of the loose-leaf auction in 1858 until today, there has been little change in the process. The farmer harvested and cured his crop; brought it to the warehouse of his choice, sometimes two or three different houses depending on the price difference or persuasive talents of warehousemen; waited in line to have his crop unloaded; visited with other farmers, neighbors and tobacco buyers; and, in the earlier days when there was not motorized transportation to get him home and back to the market before the sale the next day, enjoyed whatever entertainment was available at local nightspots. Sometimes there would be entertainment in the warehouse. But when the sale started, the farmer was most attentive. His product lay before him on the floor, and the value determined by the buyers meant success or failure. In earlier times, the start of the sale was signaled by a bugle. When the bugler sounded the opening, buyers appeared and arranged themselves on one side of the row of tobacco, and warehouse representatives arranged themselves on the other. In most cases, the warehouse owner was the sales leader, who was first in line; then came the auctioneer and, after him, other house representatives, including the man who kept track of the price, pounds and the buyer who made the purchase. As production increased and congestion in the house increased, speed of sale became a necessity.

It was incumbent on the auctioneer to keep a rapid pace and knock or "sell" a pile of tobacco to the buyer within a matter of a few seconds. The buyer also had the responsibility of judging the value of a particular pile in a flash, and of course, the sales leader should know, within close monetary range, what a particular pile of tobacco would bring. Today, a pile is sold in less than seven seconds. That rate increased over the past hundred years from about fifteen to twenty seconds per pile. If a pile of tobacco brought an unsatisfactory price, the farmer had the prerogative of turning down an edge of the identification and poundage ticket, which was placed on the pile. That told the warehouseman he wouldn't let his tobacco go for the price marked on his ticket.

Since the beginning of the auction system, there have been several periods of unrest among farmers. Even though generally accepted by all participants, the system, from time to time, has been bitterly attacked. Collusion in prices; oppression of farmers, especially when the prices were low; and favoritism of certain farmers are among some of the charges brought against the system. These ancient suspicions still surface today, even after multiple measures have been taken over the years by all sides to ensure fairness. However, leaders in the growing sectors, dealers, exporters and manufacturers alike agree that the auction method of marketing tobacco is practical in its process. From the standpoint of the farmer, it is a method wherein his commodity can be brought before a concentrated group of buyers who have access to firms that need the product for wholesale and retail demand. It is sold in an orderly fashion and with expediency to the highest bidder, and the farmer is paid within minutes.

For the most part, the charge of collusion comes, as we have said, when prices are low. When this happens, it is easy to point an accusing finger at the buyer, a tangible source. Little consideration is given by the seller to the influence of supply and demand, quality of the crop, variation in grade offering on the floor and the buyer's immediate need. After the turn of the twentieth century, many instances of cooperative marketing efforts arose as a result of farmer complaints regarding the system, but none was realized—or, if so, it failed within a short while. There are a handful of exceptions to this. Fuquay, North Carolina, hosts a cooperative market today. It is one of over three hundred warehouses in operation in the flue-cured belt.

From the buyer's standpoint, the auction system serves as a concentration of supply. The cost of buying on a community or barn-by-barn basis would be prohibitive, especially when taken into account that around three billion pounds of flue-cured tobacco are marketed annually. With the modern-day government inspection and continued display of crop in loose-leaf form, the organization, the assurance of variety and ability to fill his needs from one house to another at a rapid pace cannot be matched using any other system.

From the standpoint of the warehouse, it is a lucrative business that allows the owners to act as agents for the farmer during the selling season. It also allows the warehouseman to engage in other farm-dependent businesses, such as fertilizer, seed, chemical and crop insurance, and in many cases, he is looked upon to assist farmers with obtaining additional tobacco pounds that might be produced on the latter's farm. The communities' vested interest lies in the revenue generated by the auction sale. It is a gathering place for commerce within the county. It is where the agriculture fruits are harvested and where they are distributed among small businesses, large corporations and private operators, whose offices might be in their automobiles. The system, over the past 130 years, has proven itself to be more acceptable to all affected than any method preceding it or any method introduced by other societies after 1858.

The Auctioneer

Even with the evolutionary balance brought on by the auction concept, the resulting attraction of new community businesses spurred by the opening of a tobacco market in the villages of the flue-cured tobacco states and the importance placed on the system by the bulk of buy firms, there is another element that, unlike the others, has escaped all the problems to which the trade has been subjected: namely the tobacco auctioneer.

As previously noted, the predecessor to the auctioneer was the inspector, who came to be known as the "crier." He was paid with public funds to ensure that the purchaser received quality. With the failing credibility of the inspector and the emergence of H.B. Montague in 1827 as an independent auctioneer of integrity, the demand for a professional and private individual whose job it was to create competition among buyers began to rise. Between 1827 and the initiation of the Danville System in 1858, sales by an independent auctioneer became more numerous. However, the style of the early auctioneer, due to the lack of necessary expediency in the old market square, was executed in a lower and less theatrical mode. Also, with the exception of a few planters who brought along one of their musical and animated slaves to provide amusement to buyers and entertainment to the crowds that always gathered at the sounding of the market bell, transactions were made in a "business as usual" spirit.

With the end of the Civil War and the upswing in national demand for tobacco, plus the new loose-leaf method, market owners turned to creative ploys designed to attract more business for their warehouse. By this time, the role of the auctioneer—which in addition to selling up and down the long rows included spending most of the day standing at the big door in front of the house and sometimes out in the street, persuading passing farmers to bring their crops in to be sold in quicker time and for higher prices—was beginning to change. The theory that humor is a good attention getter proved to be successful, and with that encouragement, the auctioneer honed his talents to a fine point. After luring the farmers into the warehouse, he continued his clowning act up and down the rows as he sold the farmers' tobacco. A new and everlasting cog in the tobacco wheel was invented! The role of the auctioneer as a keen salesman, entertainer and creator of competition had permanently embedded itself into the tobacco marketing process. His act was similar to the entertainer in a medieval village festival or the barker at a street medicine show, but his purpose was a very serious one: winning customers for the warehouseman and keeping them by squeezing every dollar he could from the buyers across the row. Also, with increased demand and responding production, tobacco sales elevated to a pace much faster, both in terms of sale frequency and the need to sell a large volume in a day. This phenomenon added yet another responsibility: the ability to step up the pace to such an extent that it allowed the house to maintain fast turnover and constant product for the buyers. In the process, the warehouseman added to his own profit by selling the entire floor in a hurry, filling up and selling again. Additionally, fast-paced sales prevented warehouse congestion at a time when market towns were being flooded with farmers and their crops waiting to be sold. Not only persuasiveness but also speed and the ability to catch bidding signals from the buyers was critical in the process.

Natural entertainers and trained businessmen, auctioneers of the early period, just as today, prided themselves in being unique experts in the art of salesmanship and promoters of competitiveness on the sale. No doubt, they spent hours in private practicing colorful chants and attention-getting antics that would effectively entice exuberant competition among the bidders. Equally so, they constantly were tuned in to the crowd of onlookers, who, in more instances than not, were potential customers for the house, as well as good sources of "word-of-mouth" advertising. Those who entered this field, especially the ones who expected to be recognized as the best and ultimately most sought-after by farmers and warehousemen, continually had to seek innovative ways to draw attention to themselves and their employers.

Chiswell Dabney Langhorne, a cousin of Mark Twain (Samuel Langhorne Clemens), is recognized as the father of the modern-day tobacco auctioneer. "Chillie," as he was known by most, was a handsome gentleman from Lynchburg. At the end of the Civil War, he found himself in Danville. He was full of laughter and pranks and was constantly amusing those around him. Right after the war, he obtained employment with a local hotel as a night clerk. After spending several boring nights at the front desk, Chillie decided to have a little fun. He rang the fire bell and alerted the guests that the hotel was on fire. As the guests made their way through the lobby and out the door, he delighted in turning the water hose on them. He was immediately relieved from his duties. After this, he rounded up several nondescript horses and launched a career as the owner of a livery stable. Apparently, he was not too satisfied with this venture. It wasn't long afterward that he established the "gobble gobble" tobacco auctioneer's chant. This chant, as local legend has it, was modeled after the Gregorian chant of a Catholic priest that Langhorne heard while attending Mass with a friend in Richmond. Langhorne reasoned that the incorporation of the Gregorian chant and a staccato rhythm, along with the proper comedic antics, would draw attention to himself and the warehouse. The auctioneer who could effectively use these combinations on a tobacco sale—especially since the trend was turning to entertainment as a device to draw crowds—attract more farmers and incite buyers to higher prices became more in demand. He was an immediate success. But the job of auctioneer didn't interest Langhorne very long. He soon ventured to Richmond and established a lifetime career as a railroad man. However, this was not before his example had shown others how to draw crowds and entertain. The mold had been cut and dried for those who followed. From that point on, warehousemen made the comedy and clown factor more of a requirement for employment. This necessarily changed, to some degree, the required nature and characteristics of those who were to show interest in becoming tobacco auctioneers. Or, perhaps better stated, the newfound needs of the warehouse sale attracted more of those who were prone to entertaining and wanted to incorporate comedy into their work.

Other aspiring tobacco auctioneers immediately began to imitate the style created by Langhorne, and within a few short years, the rapid-fire chant was the norm. Those who could not quite imitate Langhorne's chant would attempt to make up the difference in other ways. In the early 1880s, Frank Barfield of Durham, North Carolina, would arrive at the warehouse dressed in flashy clothes, wearing a bright red vest and silks and carrying a brass knob walking cane. Sometimes he would blend shiny black suits with a red vest and a top hat and would stand at the warehouse door and swing his cane out to the street to attract a wagonload of tobacco headed for some other market. As sales began, he would lightly imbibe of his favorite spirits and employ an exaggerated clown act as he made his way down the neat rows of tobacco, talking to the farmers who awaited the sale and assuring them that he was the best there was and there was no need to take their tobacco crop anywhere else. When the sale started, he would twirl his cane with exuberance and entertain the buyers with laughter and his unique method of chanting for bids.

Thus, the modern-day method of chanting began: skillfully taking the bid, pushing up the price and prodding the buyers to squeeze just one more penny per pound. Aside from Langhorne, the architect of the modern chant, and Captain Parrish, who as we noted earlier combined his talents as preacher and bartender into auctioneering, other prominent names of the nineteenth and early twentieth centuries share in the molding of today's auctioneer. Among them is Captain A.J. "Buck" Ellington, who began auctioning at Piedmont Warehouse in Reidsville in 1875. Ellington was known for his fine voice and considered to be one of the best tobacco auctioneers in the South. He was often referred to as a "power on a tobacco sale."

Washington Duke had built the first tobacco factory in Durham after the Civil War, and he and his sons had gone after the tobacco trade in America with unprecedented aggressiveness. To a large degree, the Dukes played the leading role in introducing tobacco markets to areas other than Virginia, Maryland and North Carolina. By the turn of the twentieth century, tobacco was being produced in South Carolina, Georgia, Florida, Kentucky, Tennessee, Louisiana and Missouri. The success of the Dukes accomplished, among other things, more widespread use of tobacco and keener competition from the other tobacco dealers. The ultimate result was a larger demand for the new raw product and, of course, the need for warehouses in new production areas. This expanded the demand for tobacco auctioneers. Sixty years after Chiswell Dabney Langhorne formulated the model for the rapid-fire chant in selling tobacco, heirs to that chant had hashed and rehashed it on the warehouse floor to the extent that, while the basics were still there, it was fine-tuned to the art we hear on the sales floor today.

Langhorne, Parrish, Ellington and all who succeeded them into the 1990s would be classified as amateurs compared to the professionals of today. Most auctioneers knew one another and, in most cases, were friends. In those days, as is the case today, they were a close-knit family. Auctioneers who came along at the turn of the twentieth century were influenced by those who started out behind Langhorne. Garland Webb displayed the Langhorne form at Farmers Warehouse in Durham in 1883 and, later, in Winston-Salem and the coastal plains areas. Others were Mat Nelson and John C. Neal of Danville, the latter being the son of Thomas D. Neal, one of the originators of the loose-leaf auction system; John Abe Newson of Winston-Salem; Francis Hicks of Henderson; Keaton Watkins of Warrenton; and "Tug" Wilson and Captain Tom Washington of Wilson. Some historians have characterized the auctioneer as a kind of official jester for entertaining the crowd.

Although his more serious duty required that he set the pace for sales, he was always a jovial fellow given to spectacular performances but never failing to interpret the winks, nods, salutes or out-stuck tongues of the buyers, who often raised bids by such signals. It must be understood that, even though over the past one hundred years in which the tobacco auctioneer has earned the reputation of being hard living, fast talking, light-hearted and funny, there is a very serious side that prevails. Through all the antics, this man is an important businessman. It is his responsibility to know the quality of tobacco on the warehouse floor, to know which of the eight to eleven buyers across the rows is interested in a certain quality or grade being offered at the moment and how much they might bid. He must keep up with who is bidding in competition; he must keep the farmer (the customer) in mind, and he must know when to "knock" the pile of tobacco out to a buyer. This responsibility comes while he is chanting at the rate of three to five hundred words a minutes and selling a pile of tobacco every five to seven seconds. Anywhere from $150 to $400 is turned over on the warehouse floor when a pile is sold. That adds up to hundreds of thousands of dollars per day. So, one can see that this jovial entertainer is also astute in conducting serious business.

GUNFIRE ON THE AUCTION FLOOR?

Sometimes the pressure got quite intense. Harold "High Dollar" Daniels told of an incident in the 1950s when he had to deal with one particular buyer who, for one reason or another, couldn't be satisfied. He had a habit of frequently stopping the sale and complaining. "I kept telling him that he was getting on my nerves and that if he didn't straighten up and quit stopping the sale that I was gonna break him sooner or later," he said.

> *He wouldn't listen, though, so one morning I stuck a pistol that fired blanks in my pocket, and when he started in on me again, I warned him. Finally, I told him if he messed with me again, I was gonna shoot him. He didn't believe it. He kept right on. In the middle of the row, he started whining. I reached in my pocket and pulled that owl head special out and BANG, I shot him. He fell right across the row. He thought he was dead for sure. The other folks on the sale knew what I was doing, and they all killed themselves laughing. From that day on, he left me alone, and we were friends.*

BIBLIOGRAPHY

"About Altria," December 1, 2006. http://www.altria.com/about_altria/1_7_ aboutaltriafaq.asp.

Algeo, Katie. "The Rise of Tobacco as a Southern Appalachian Staple: Madison County, North Carolina." *Southeastern Geographer* 37 (May 197): 46–60.

Bowman, D.R., and H.E. Heggestad. "Burley Tobacco Quality, Yield and Chemical Composition as Affected by the Time of Harvest." *University of Tennessee Agricultural Experiment Station Bulletin* 230 (March 1953).

Brooks, James. "Tobacco Farmers Turning Over New Leaf with Different System." *Johnson City (TN) Press*, September 27, 2005.

Brooks, Jerome. *The Mighty Leaf*. Boston: Little, Brown and Company, 1952.

Brown, Blake, and Will Snell. "Policy Issues Surrounding Tobacco Quota Buyout Legislation." North Carolina State University and University of Kentucky, 2003.

Brown & Williamson Tobacco Corporation. *Tobacco...Working for America*. Louisville, KY: Brown & Williamson, 1994–95.

Bulletins of the (U.S.) Bureau of Plant Industry. Nos. 241–47. Washington, D.C.: Government Printing Office, 1912.

Burley Stabilization Corporation. *52 Years of Service to Tobacco Farmers*. Knoxville, TN: Burley Stabilization Corporation, 2005.

Burt, Thomas, blues singer. Tape-recorded interview by author, June 4, 1989. Durham, NC.

Cage, Bob, tobacco auctioneer. Tape-recorded interview by author, January 1, 1989. South Boston, VA.

Chance, Frank. "Daily Farm Operations of University of Tennessee Tobacco Experiment Station, 1932–1936." Unpublished diary.

Chapman, E.J., R.L. Davis, J.H. Felts, B.C. Nichols and W.L. Parks. "Response of Burley Tobacco to Irrigation and Nitrogen." *University of Tennessee Agricultural Experiment Station Bulletin* 368 (October 1963).

Chase, Morgan J.P. Personal communication, 2007.

———. Telephone interviews. January 26 and 31, 2007.

Clayton, E.E., and H.E. Heggestad. "Burley 1A: A New Black Root Rot Resistant Tobacco." *University of Tennessee Agricultural Experiment Station Bulletin* 106 (February 1951).

Clayton, E.E., H.E. Heggestad, M.O. Neas and H.A. Skoog. "Development of Burley 21: The First Wildfire Resistant Tobacco Variety." *University of Tennessee Agricultural Experiment Station Bulletin* 321 (December 1960).

Coscarelli, Anne. "The Truth about Lung Cancer and the People Who Get It." *UCLA Today* 26, no. 12 (2006). Available online at http://www.today.ucla.edu/2006/060411voices_lung_cancer.html.

Cotton, Lee Pelham. "Tobacco: Colonial Cultivation Methods." Fact sheet prepared for distribution at Colonial (Virginia) National Historical Park, U.S. National Park Service. 1998.

Daniels, Harold, tobacco auctioneer. Tape-recorded interview by author, October 14, 1988. Nelson, VA.

Danville Tobacco Association, Inc. *100 Years of Progress*. Danville, VA: Danville Tobacco Association, Inc., 1969.

Farm Service Agency. *Burley Tobacco Quota Program*. Washington, D.C.: United States Department of Agriculture, 2004.

———. "Tobacco Transition Payment Program: Fact Sheet." 2005. http://www.fsa.usda.gov/pas/publications/facts/html/ttpp05.htm.

Finger, William R. *The Tobacco Industry in Transition*. Lexington, MA: Lexington Books, 1981.

Forty-fourth Annual Report of the Agricultural Experiment Station of the University of Tennessee, for 1931. Knoxville: University of Tennessee, 1931.

Garner, Wightman Wells, Charles Walter Bacon and Charles Lon Foubert. "Research Studies on the Curing of Leaf Tobacco." *Bulletin of the U.S. Department of Agriculture* 79 (April 23, 1914).

General Accounting Office. "Tobacco Settlement: States' Use of Master Settlement Payments." 2001. file://A:\master settlement.htm.

Grise, Verner, and Karen Griffin. *U.S. Tobacco Industry: Background of the Tobacco Program*. Agricultural Economic Report Number 589. Washington, D.C.: United States Department of Agriculture, Economic Research Service, 1988.

Hayes, Hank. "Jenkins: Debate Needed on Cigarette Oversight." *Johnson City (TN) Press*, October 17, 2004. Available online at http://www.johnsoncitypress.com/Printstory.asp.

Heggestad, H.E., and M.O. Neas. "Burley 11A and 11B: The Disease Resistant Varieties." *University of Tennessee Agricultural Experiment Station Bulletin* 261 (June 1957).

———. "Burley 2: A New Improved Variety of Tobacco." *University of Tennessee Agricultural Experiment Station Bulletin* 110 (March 1953).

Heggestad, H.E., L.J. Hoffbeck, M.O. Neas and H.A. Skoog. "Burley 49: A New Disease Resistant Burley Tobacco." *University of Tennessee Agricultural Experiment Station Bulletin* 395 (July 1965).

Heggestad, H.E., M.O. Neas and H.A. Skoog. "Burley 37: A Black Shank and Wildfire Resistant Burley Tobacco." *University of Tennessee Agricultural Experiment Station Bulletin* 333 (October 1961).

Henningfield, Jack. *Nicotine: An Old Fashion Addiction*. New York: Chelsea House Publishers, 1985.

Herndon, Melvin. *Historical Booklet No. 20*. Williamsburg, VA: Jamestown 350th Anniversary Celebration Corporation, 1957.

Heyes, Eileen. *Tobacco U.S.A.: The Industry Behind the Smoke Curtain*. Brookfield, CT: Twenty-first Century Books, 1999.

Howard, Donald, superintendent, University of Tennessee Tobacco Experiment Station, 1974–1981. Response to questionnaire, April 4, 1990. Jackson, TN.

Jarrett, William T. "The Burley Tobacco Buyout Program and Its Impact on Farmers in Tennessee, Virginia, and North Carolina." Electronic Theses and Dissertations. Paper 2039, 2007. http://dc.etsu.edu/etd/2039.

Jolliff, Jimmy, tobacco auctioneer. Tape-recorded interview by author, July 20, 1988, Smithfield, NC.

Killebrew, J.B., and Herbert Myrick. *Tobacco Leaf: Its Culture and Cure, Marketing and Manufacture*. New York: Orange Judd Company, 1910.

Kuiper, Koenrad, and Frederick Tillis. "The Chant of the Tobacco Auctioneer." *American Speech* 60, no. 2 (1985).

Lung Cancer Report. "How Common Is Lung Cancer?" December 17, 2006. http://www.review-and-compare.com/Treat-yourself/Lung-Cancer.aspx.

McGee, Barry. "R.J. Reynolds Tobacco Company." In *Encyclopedia of North Carolina*. Chapel Hill: University of North Carolina Press, 2006.

Miller, Robert D. "TN 86: A Burley Tobacco Resistant to TVMV, TEV, and PVY." *University of Tennessee Agricultural Experiment Station Bulletin* 657 (October 1987).

Parker-Pope, Tara. *Cigarettes: Anatomy of an Industry from Seed to Smoke*. New York: New Press, 2001.

Phase II Settlement Administration Services. "What's the Difference? Phase I vs. Phase II." 2006. http://ncphase2.wcsr.com/pdfs/PhaseI_vsPhaseII_brochure.pdf.

Ray, Daryll. "Is a Tobacco Buyout on the Horizon?" Agricultural Policy Analysis Center, April 19, 2002. http://apacweb.ag.utk.edu/weekcol/091.html.

Reaves, Dixie W. "Virginia Cooperative Extension." Unpublished ms., Virginia Tech, 2005. Available online at http://www.ext.vt.edu/news/periodicals/fmu/2005-10/impacts.html.

Robert, Joseph. *The Tobacco Kingdom*. Gloucester, MA, 1965.

Sieber, Samantha. "It's Just Too Dry." *Bristol Herald Courier*, December 1, 2005.

Silliman, Sherwood, American Tobacco Company. Letter to L.A. "Speed" Riggs, tobacco auctioneer, December 21, 1937. Letter in possession of author.

Singh, Ajay. "To Your Health: The Silent Killer." *UCLA Today* 25, no. 3 (2004). Available online at http://www.today.ucla.edu/2004/04102campus_yourhealth.html.

Tobacco Institute. *Tennessee and Tobacco: A Chapter in America's Industrial Growth*. Washington, D.C.: Tobacco Institute, 1972.

———. *Virginia's Tobacco Heritage*. Washington, D.C.: Tobacco Institute, 1985.

Tiller, Kelly. Personal communication, October 4, 2006; November 14, 2006; January 7, 2007.

—————. *Tennessee Tobacco Master Settlement Agreement.* Knoxville, TN: University of Tennessee Agricultural Policy Analysis Center, 2000.

—————. *Tobacco Buyout "Top Ten": A List of Things You Should Know About the Buyout.* Knoxville, TN: University of Tennessee Agricultural Policy Analysis Center, 2005.

—————. *Tobacco Production in Tennessee: An Economic Perspective.* Knoxville, TN: University of Tennessee Agricultural Policy Analysis Center, 2000.

—————. "Use of Phase II in Other Major Tobacco States." 2001.

—————. "Use of Phase II Payments in Tennessee." 2001. http://apacweb.ag.utk. edu/tobacco/pu2001marchphase2tn.pdf.

—————. "Use of Tobacco Settlement Payments in Other Major Tobacco States." 2001.

—————. "Use of Tobacco Settlement Payments in Tennessee." 2001. http:// apacweb.ag.edu/tobacco/pu2001marchmsatn.pdf.

Tiller, Kelly, William Snell and Blake Brown. "Tobacco Buyout Information: What Is the Tobacco Quota Buyout?" 2006.

Tilley, Nannie May. *The Bright Tobacco Industry.* Chapel Hill: University of North Carolina Press, 1948.

United States Department of Agriculture. *Tobacco: United States and State Estimates, 1866–1965.* Washington, D.C.: Government Printing Office, 1970.

Vandiver, J.L. "Daily Farm Operations of University of Tennessee Tobacco Experiment Station, 1936–1938." Unpublished diary.

Virginia Farm Bureau. Farm Bureau "News and Features." November 3, 2005.

Virginia Tobacco Settlement Foundation. "The History of the Virginia Tobacco Settlement Foundation." 2006.

Womach, Jasper. "Tobacco Quota Buyout." 2004. http://64.233.187.104/ search?q=cache:GWEtJvX5iaYJ:www.uky.edu/Ag.

INDEX

ABOUT THE AUTHORS

W.W. "Billy" Yeargin Jr. is an international authority on tobacco. He lives in Selma, North Carolina. A native of Oxford, North Carolina, Yeargin is the author of *North Carolina Tobacco: A History* and *Remembering North Carolina Tobacco*. He has been involved in the activities of the Duke Homestead Historical Site and the Oak Ridge Military Academy. He spent much of his career in leadership roles with grower organizations, including tobacco growers and sweet potato growers. He graduated from the University of North Carolina and earned a master's degree from Duke University. He later studied at the University of Oxford, England.

Christopher Evans Bickers is an independent journalist living in Raleigh, North Carolina. He specializes in agricultural reporting, especially on tobacco, and has been published frequently in such magazines as *Southeast Farm Press*, *Progressive Farmer* and *Tobacco International*. Born in Greenville, South Carolina, he was raised in Memphis and Knoxville, Tennessee, and graduated from the University of Tennessee (Knoxville), where he majored in history. He received a master's degree in journalism from the University of Georgia. He currently writes and publishes *Tobacco Farmer Newsletter*.